JUSTICE RESTORED

THE GARY GEIGER & WAYNE BLANCHARD STORY

Dr. Thomas Frank Christian

Portland • Oregon

Gary Geiger's compelling journey from victim to survivor to advocate following his mediation with his offenders is chronicled in *Justice Restored*. Gary has shared his story with victims of crime, advocates and with offenders incarcerated in a number of New york State's correctional and youth facilities as he promotes restorative justice for victims, offenders and the community.

Gary Hook
Division of Children and Families
New York State Office of Mental Health
Albany , New York

With *Justice Restored*, Dr. Christian shares a powerful story that can help both victims heal and offenders be accounable. Thank you, Doctor, for lighting a candle in a criminal justice world full of darkness.

Patrick Joseph Mulvehill, MA, M. Ed.
Psychologist, Retired
Saint Paul, Minnesota

*To Gary Geiger
and Wayne Blanchard
for sharing their story*

ACKNOWLEDGMENTS

I would like to thank the following people for their help and support in putting together this book: my wife Bernice; my son Craig and his wife Laura; my son Andy; my daughter Jen; Gary Geiger, Wayne Blanchard, Angela Blanchard, Goldie Jackson, and Ramel A. Eaddy, Gary Smith and Tommy Brown for sharing their life experiences; New York State Chief Judge Judith S. Kaye and Chief Administrative Judge Jonathan Lippman and former Chief Administrator of the New York Courts, Matthew Crossen for their support and leadership; my former New York State dispute resolution staff: Mark Collins, Yvonne Taylor and Tom Buckner; Howard Zehr, Mark Umbreit and Dennis Wittman for their dialogue and sharing over the years on restorative justice and victim and offender mediation; all the New York correctional personnel, especially former New York State Corrections Commissioner Thomas Coughlin (deceased), James Flateau, Director of Public Information, Superintendent of Eastern Correctional Facility, William Mitchel, and corrections counselor Mark Ackerhalt; Gaby Monet and her Home Box Office film crew; Alice Heiserman and her staff at the American Correctional Association; Peggy Wells and Jen Christian (again) for their editing assistance; my neighbors Gail and Dave Smith for their back up computer; and Morgan Durant for his computer expertise.

CHAPTERS

PREFACE

This is a true story. It initially involves two people's lives. One is a victim who is shot in a robbery and the other is the person who shot him. As time passed, this incident would affect many lives in the state of New York and, with the help of the print and television media, people around the world. It is such a powerful story that I have been asked many times after presentations and victim and offender training to record it in book form so it can be shared in its entirety by an even wider audience. This is a story that will describe the horrors of crime and the devastation it can cause to victims, their families and their communities. It also focuses on the perpetrators of crime and how their own behavior limits their lives and the consequences it causes for the people around them. Lastly, it proposes a new look at justice in our society. This approach questions how retribution or punishment alone can find and restore justice for anyone. The Gary Geiger and Wayne Blanchard story demonstrates that through mediation and a restorative justice approach, a sense of equity can be achieved for both the victim and the offender and their worlds.

JUSTICE RESTORED

CHAPTER ONE

THE CRIME

On August 13, 1981, two young men were sitting outside Arthur's Round Table, a bar on Northern Boulevard and 2nd Avenue in Albany, New York. It had been a warm summer day, and they were drinking alcohol and smoking marijuana weed. It was getting late and they had just run out of money. Bars were open till 4 a.m. in New York, so without the proper finances, it was time to leave and go back to work. Work for them was a little unconventional. It involved putting a gun in someone's face and taking his money. It was faster than burglary, and there was no wait to fence any stolen merchandise.

Albany is the capitol of the Empire State and is 150 miles from the Big Apple, New York City. One of the young men was visiting a lady friend in Albany and figured it was about time to make a score and return to his home in the City. As they pondered their options, a station wagon pulled up to the curb and a young teenager jumped out. Three other young men stayed in the car. The new arrival approached his friends and detailed a scheme that could total 50,000 dollars if all worked out according to plan. He had cased the Best Western Motel down by the bus depot and had spotted a safe in the back room. The word was that weeks of lodging transactions from legislators, state workers and tourist visitors now sat in that safe. It was ripe for the taking, and they could peel it open and all be on easy street.

The New Yorker was skeptical. Why would these young punks want to include him and his friend in on their find? His partner had no hesitation. He was a local and had a reputation on the streets as one tough player. He knew the young men and figured they needed the experience of veteran stickup men, and although he was on parole from a previous prison bit (sentence) for robbery, he was definitely in. He got up in a hurry and announced that he was on his way to his crib (house) to get his piece (gun).

The station wagon was soon proceeding down State Street loaded with the six young men. It was 3:00 a.m. The driver was being cautious and tried to drive slowly in order not to draw too much attention to them. This was his mother's car, and he was not too sure he should be part of this escapade anyway. The New Yorker pulled his piece out of his pocket waved the gun and gave the orders. All listened intently. The driver would stay with the car and be ready for a quick getaway. One of the young teenagers would stay by the door and warn them if a police car or somebody else spelling trouble came by. The four others would enter the main lobby of the hotel. The leader would approach the night auditor and ask about room rates. One of the teenagers would go to the bar side and the other experienced robber would cover the garage entrance. The two teenagers would act like jitterbugs and pretend to get into a verbal argument to distract the night clerk. The leader would then leap over the counter and put his weapon in the face of the lone night auditor. Two others would come around the counter and overpower the clerk. They would tip the till and then have the "chump" open the safe. The plan was in place and they were ready to make it come together.

The car pulled up to the Best Western Motel. The motel sat down the hill in the shadow of the New York State

Capitol Building. Next to the motel was the bus depot. It was not the best part of town, but it was convenient for people on state business. It took a state rate and was also used by tourists to the Capitol and the Empire State Plaza just up the hill. The Empire State Plaza was made up of five majestic buildings erected under former Governor Nelson A. Rockefeller. Rocky served as governor from 1958 to 1973. The story on the Empire State Plaza was that the Governor was embarrassed when Princess Beatrix of the Netherlands came for a visit. Albany was a former Dutch settlement and the Princess wanted to see the Capitol and the city of Albany. The Capitol was a magnificent architectural masterpiece, but the area around it was made up of old buildings and looked pretty ragged. The Governor decided to have the old buildings torn down and the Empire State Plaza plans were developed. People were put out of their homes and many old brownstones went down to please the Governor. A few houses of prostitution also were victims, and as in the olden days, they could no longer serve the visiting politicians and their friends. The Governor, shortly after the royalty's visit, had the Empire State Plaza built so the next esteemed visitor would be duly impressed by the Capitol and the surrounding area. Four twenty story state office buildings were constructed along with a state library, museum and theater. The theater was in the shape of a large egg and was made of poured concrete. A true marvel to behold! The Best Western Motel was a carryover from the old neighborhood. It had survived the Governor's wrecking ball but it was now about to be robbed.

The four young men nonchalantly sashayed into the motel. The night clerk addressed the two asking about a room, and in a sweeping motion, surveyed the others standing at the inside doors. His face displayed the reality that he knew he was about to be robbed. He had a short-sleeved shirt on and his arms bulged with muscle. He had lifted some weights in his day, and his new arrivals knew he may be someone to be reckoned with before the night was over. The clerk looked one way and saw one of the perpetrators had come through the back office door. As he looked at him, his eyes went down to his hand. He saw a silver plated revolver pointed in his direction. His instincts were right. "This is a stick up," the young bandit said. The victim turned the other way, and the two in front of him leaped over the counter. They told him to get down. A slight hesitation on his part brought a barrage of fists, kicks and a pistol whipping. They meant business. As he sank to the floor, his glasses were ripped off, cutting the inside of his eye. The pistol butt to the temple opened a severe gash to his head. He was bleeding profusely, as head wounds do, and everything looked fuzzy to him. Now that they had his attention, they placed the gun to his head. They just wanted the money, they said. He pointed out the money- box under the counter. They also tore his back pocket and took his billfold. Because the motel was in a rough part of town, he only carried ten dollars on him when he came to work. Total take so far with the money - box and the clerk's billfold was 150 dollars. The other gun wielder announced that he had seen the safe in the inner office. Bingo! The real purpose of the evening's work was now at hand. The night clerk was backed into that office and the gun was again placed to his head. The message was clear. "Open the safe, Jack." There was one small hitch. The night auditor said he didn't have the combination. It was known only by the manager and he was upstairs sleeping in another room in the motel. The night auditor would pay a price for his shortcomings. He was hit by the butt of the gun and fists and kicked as he went down for the second time. The gun was again placed to his head. He tried to convince the intruders that he was telling the truth. He explained again to them that he was cooperating as much as he could, but the safe was something he had no power over.

The word came down, hit him over the head and let's blow this "pop stand." The butt of the gun cracked up aside the back of his head again as he lay on the shag carpet in the office. This time he looked like he was knocked out. His face was buried in the carpet and he didn't move. The four perpetrators ran out over the linoleum floor in the lobby, and picking up their look out, raced for the waiting car. The clerk could hear their footsteps on the noisy surface. He had been playing possum and now it was over. He had survived. He jumped to his feet, thinking he had to run the other way to call for help. But as the New Yorker had gone out the door, he turned to his partner and motioned for him to check one more time to make sure the night auditor was really out of commission. They wanted time for a clean getaway. "Do what you have to do" was the nonverbal communication. As the partner looked in, the night auditor had just gotten up. The silver plated revolver was raised quickly and pointed at his back. A loud cannon like shot rang out. The bullet tore through the night auditor's back, piercing his right lung, breaking three ribs and bouncing to a halt deep in his stomach muscle. He started to run towards a closed door and hit it and spun as he fell. The shooter turned and ran.

The five "perps" piled into the car and the driver again drove slowly away. They wanted to know if the clerk had been shot. " I think I hit him," was the response. Now the New Yorker was getting nervous and wanted the wheelman to speed it up a little. The driver said it was better to continue to proceed at a normal pace. He went directly to his mother's house. They split up the money. The total take was still only 150 dollars. It was a long way from $50,000. The New York connection said it was "chump change" and he didn't even want his share. That made 30 dollars apiece. Not a very good day's work. They figured it was better than nothing but a high price to pay if the clerk died. All took off trying to get lost and fade into the streets of Albany.

At first, the night auditor didn't realize that he had been shot. He had felt a burning sensation in his back, but in the excitement of the moment his first thoughts were to summon help. He made a quick call to his manager in the second floor motel room and then he called the bus-station next door. People came running from all directions. There was no 911 emergency number to call in those days, but the police and ambulance squad response time was still excellent. As the police tried to gather information from the clerk, the paramedics placed him on a couch and tended to his head wounds. One paramedic noticed blood dripping through the back of the man's sweater. As they pulled up his clothing, the clerk turned and saw for the first time blood running down his back. The loud cannon like explosion had been gunfire and the shooter had been on target. He had been shot and was in serious condition. The commotion and excitement were running high. The victim was starting to go into a state of shock. He was having trouble breathing due to the excruciating pain so they gave him oxygen. He couldn't give the police much help except to say four young Black men had held him up. It was time to rush him to the Albany Medical Center emergency room.

The police put out a radio dispatch to all Albany police cars, the Albany County Sheriff's Department, neighboring law enforcement agencies and the New York State Police to look for what they thought were four young armed and dangerous robbers. All State Thruway ticket booths were notified to be on the lookout for four suspicious men heading, most likely, to New York City. The perpetrators were either on the streets of Albany or on their way back to the Big Apple. That was the normal method of operation. The police were confident. They would catch these "perps", hopefully sooner than later. Not to worry. The "dog watch" (midnight to eight a.m. shift) was just getting interesting.

CHAPTER TWO

THE VICTIM

The night auditor at the Best Western Motel early that fateful August morning was a thirty-four year old man by the name of Gary Geiger. He was from Scotia, New York, a suburb of Albany. He had chosen to work the 11 p.m. to 7 a.m. graveyard shift at the motel so he could pursue his track career and train during the day. He had placed fourth in his age group in the 45-meter dash at the National Championships in 1980. In 1981, he had visions of improving his times and attracting the attention of the media, and maybe gaining the sponsorship of a shoe company with the ultimate goal of landing a coaching position in track at a local high school or community college. In high school he had been a small 118-pound teenager. He had begun to lift weights in his twenties to build himself up and improve his self-image. He was so focused in his efforts that by the age of thirty, he had become a nationally ranked power lifter. All his athletic ability, his muscles and his speed were no help to him now. He had been beaten, pistol whipped, humiliated and shot. He was now simply another crime victim.

Gary Geiger was rushed into the emergency room to face a possible operation to remove the bullet. After the x-rays, the doctor explained to him that he was a very lucky man. The 22-caliber bullet had entered his back, passed through his right lung, broken three ribs and lodged in his abdomen. His weight lifting had developed his stomach muscles to the point that they literally stopped the bullet. Just like Superman! The normal path of a 22-shell trajectory is to bounce around and do extensive internal damage to vital organs. Gary Geiger's conditioning had prevented that. Gary's mother and sister were now at the hospital. Tears came to his eyes as he saw his family and their concern. He was beginning to realize all that had happened to him. The doctor said that at this stage, he recommended they not operate. The bullet was so deep in the muscle tissue that it would do more damage to cut into the muscle than to let it alone. He couldn't guarantee that the bullet would not move, but right now, the x-rays showed it was stationary. If he was lucky, he might be walking around with a bullet in him for the rest of his life.

The police were at his bedside trying to have him describe the robbers and look at mug shots. Gary was in no shape to be of any help. He couldn't describe his assailants, and his glasses that were torn off his face in the confrontation were still at the scene of the crime. A detective retrieved his glasses and brought them to his hospital room. Looking over the pictures, he still could not give them any type of description except that they were four young Black men. He was stressed out and his nerves were jumpy. He was emotionally drained. He had come this close to being killed or paralyzed for life. He worried that the bullet that had bounced around in his body would move and he would be in the operating room any minute.

Gary stayed in the hospital for only two days and then was released with the bullet still in his body. If it were to move, they would have him return and begin to probe to see if they could find the bullet and remove it. He had run the 45-meter sprints in record time on the track, but now he had trouble walking from his chair to the bathroom.

The police again had him look at photos of possible

suspects, but everything was still a blur. As nighttime came, Gary began to relive the robbery. He would wake up in a cold sweat. He was dreaming of being robbed, and eerily, it was as if it was happening all over again. This is what happens to many crime victims. Their whole body reacts as it did the first time they were victimized. The emotional and psychological damage is draining. As he paced in the dark, he realized that as he relived the horror, he could actually see the faces of his tormentors clearly. The next morning, he called the detectives and said he thought he could identify the robbers. The police brought him down to the station and he picked out the New Yorker and his Albany partner as soon as he saw their pictures. Arrest warrants were issued for a Goldie Jackson, alias Jay Dee Walker, a known parolee, and a Wayne Blanchard, another local parolee released from prison only four months previously. The method of operation (M.O.) for both suspects "holding up people," a.k.a....robbers.

After a few days, Gary Geiger felt better. One of the suspects, Goldie Jackson had been arrested, and there was an all-points bulletin out on the other, Wayne Blanchard. The wheelman was given up by Goldie Jackson. His name was Ramel Eaddy.

Gary needed to go back to work to be able to pay his bills and get on with his life. He called the Best Western Motel to let them know that he thought he was ready to resume his job. He asked to be put on days for obvious reasons. They informed him that the main office had decided that Gary was to be laid off. There had been too much publicity and they did not want him back. They would, however, put him in for unemployment compensation. In so many words, he was now out of work. In 1981, there was not a whole lot he could do about the company's decision. He realized that he could not afford his car payments nor his present rent. He had been staying with his mother until he felt better. He now had to move into the local Y.M.C.A. He was a true victim of crime. He did not have insurance so no counselor would help him with his post-traumatic stress. He had no automobile, no job and his new companions at the Y offered him alcohol and drugs to cope with his pain. He turned them down, but at one point, he pulled his last quarter out of his pocket and thought it wasn't just the Best Western Motel that had been robbed. He had been stripped of everything he held as important in his life. He would have to rely on his mother and sister until he could regroup and start again. He could do that. He had done that before in his life.

While attending high school in Schenectady, New York, in the mid sixties, Gary Geiger would pass Pat Riley, then a senior, on a daily basis in the hallway between class breaks. Riley who went on to play professional basketball and is known as one of the best National Basketball Association coaches, was a star athlete in three sports in high school. Geiger often wondered if he could ever emulate Pat Riley, be like Pat, be somebody.

Geiger's earlier home life in high school had been tumultuous. His father went from job to job and had become an alcoholic. His mother attempted to keep the family together by working two jobs, and she spent many nights arguing with her husband, trying to get him to assume his responsibilities as a spouse and father. This stressful atmosphere had a profound effect on Gary and his sister. It would have an enduring and lasting repercussion on him for years to come.

While in high school, he resumed his track running, which he had participated in during junior high school. During his three years in high school, he ran the 100 yard, 220 yard and the 4 X 220 yard relay. His goal was to beat his dad's times when his dad was a star sprinter in high school. He tied his 220-yard time but not his 100-yard time. His dad never let him forget it, and this helped perpetuate Gary's low self-esteem. But it also started an inner fire, which had kept Gary going through tough times. It gave him a motivation, a desire to succeed and never quit, even in the face of adversity. His teen years would make him tough, to the point that he felt he could survive anything. He had nurtured those skills, and the day had come when he would need them all to save his life.

Gary played church basketball in the winter and ran his track in the spring and fall. His high school years were pretty mundane. He had transferred from one school district to another before his first year of high school and the majority of his old friends attended the rival school, so he often felt alienated and an outsider, another emotion he would be familiar with when he became a crime victim. The one thing that he was most proud of was being instrumental in helping his relay team set a sectional record, thus qualifying for the New York State high school championships. To his regret, however, his father did not attend the meet and this added more distance between them. Four months after the event, Gary's father died suddenly, leaving his surviving family with virtually nothing but tears and anger. His death and the almost non-existent relationship they had, would haunt Gary for years. His family would now have to pick up the pieces and slowly move on in the hopes of finding themselves.

After graduating from high school, Gary decided to attend a two-year community college located near his home. He majored in accounting and took a course in public speaking, which would serve him well in the future. The course also helped him with his shyness and it led him to be able to meet his first girlfriend. He did well in school, receiving A's in accounting, English and public speaking. During the summer months, he worked for a local bank as a messenger and later was promoted to a bank teller. He gained a lot of confidence from the community college and decided to try his hand at a four-year college. He transferred his credits to a college in Bangor, Maine. This would prove to be a mistake in more ways than one.

To help pay for his tuition in Maine, he took out a student loan from the bank where he had worked during the summer. The loan was for more than the tuition and room and board, so he now had a car, plenty of spending money and a whole new set of friends. He went from a nobody to a very popular guy overnight. Gary got caught up in a wild student life style of the day and night. He rarely attended class, partied from dusk to dawn, took trips to Boston on a whim and somehow lasted the first year. During the next summer while working at the bank, he received a letter from the college stating that he was academically ineligible for the fall semester. He promptly procured another loan from his bank, drove to Bangor in September, paid his tuition and was immediately declared eligible to return. He learned another lesson about the power of money.

Gary also got caught up in a trick of student crime. He would go into a supermarket, stash cartons of cigarettes under his coat and go back to campus and sell them at a discount rate. With his luck, he tried it once and was apprehended and turned in by the merchant. He was arrested, fingerprinted, prosecuted and fined one hundred dollars. The offense was a misdemeanor and would not be on his record. He could claim he had never been arrested for a felony and would not have to put it on any employment form. But he learned a valuable lesson and decided that he did not want to be involved in the criminal justice system.

Gary's money was now running out and so were his so called friends. The Vietnam War was beginning to escalate and rumors were running wild on campus that students not doing too well in the classroom were being drafted. He talked to his sister and she informed him that the local reserve unit in Schenectady, New York, was forming a first come, first served unit, and it might be a good idea if he joined up.

One night after partying in a pub near campus, he excused himself, drove his car back to his dorm, filled his automobile with his belongings and headed back home without telling a soul. Two days later he started his six-year stint in the United States Army Reserves. Being in the reserves meant that a person has to go to the basic and advanced training for six months, then go to monthly meetings and every summer go to an army base for two weeks. During Gary's basic training, two events occurred which would help shape the rest of his life. He had always prided himself in being in tip-top physical condition; however, his time in college had dissipated his condition and the years of neglect had taken their toll. His basic training maneuvers were a wake up call. One early February morning after a forced march, he looked up at the bright moon and promised himself that he would never let himself get out of shape again. He wanted to be in control of his own body and his own life. Another value he learned from his basic military training was discipline. He was determined to be organized, punctual and have a plan for his future. He set out to work through his plan for his daily life. It was a value that would serve him well after his victimization.

Upon returning home from his basic and advanced training, Gary went back to the bank to work full time. He started as a teller and was soon promoted to a loan teller and then into a new position as a systems analyst. He was moving up the ladder quickly, perhaps too swiftly. At this time, he was developing a relationship with a young lady who worked at one of the branch offices of the bank. The relationship became very serious, and Gary tried to balance his new responsibilities with the relationship. The stress became too much to handle, and the relationship ended. It wasn't too long after that, the bank position also ended. Gary did not like the banking image nor the atmosphere that seemed to encompass his entire life. He wanted control over his life and not a job that dictated his every move.

For the next few years, Gary drifted in and out of jobs, trying to find his niche in life. In the early 70's, he also started to weight train to look better and to build up his self-esteem. He found out that not only did he enjoy it, but he had become the strongest person in the local gym. He decided to enter local and regional power lifting competitions. It wasn't long before he was placing in the top three in his weight class every time he competed. He was now addicted to lifting weights and it was all he wanted to do.

In 1978, Gary started to work for the Best Western Motel in Albany, New York, as the head bookkeeper. Within a year, he was promoted to traveling auditor. His territory included Albany; Cranston, Rhode Island; Philadelphia, Pennsylvania; and Newark, Delaware. It was a lonely job traveling to each city, auditing the books and having employees ostracize you for fear of losing their jobs. Nobody likes someone looking over their shoulders, much less their bookkeeping methods. During one audit, he caught the motel manager dipping into the petty cash fund. The manager was fired, and the next day, Gary went to his car and it did not start. He lifted the hood and found the battery was missing.

In each city where he went to perform an audit, he made it a point to visit the local gym. Whenever he piled on the weights, a crowd would gather and encourage him and help spot the weights so he could keep increasing the volume. They would then ask him questions about his routine and make him feel like a celebrity. He was beginning to feel an identity. His confidence was growing and he was now sure of himself. He was not worried anymore about his future. The life expectancy of a traveling hotel auditor job is about six months. The burn out rate is high. Gary lasted the average time. The job had its benefits but the constant traveling wore on him. Beginning in 1978 and into 1979, Gary's Spartan lifestyle would end. He was entering and winning power lifting competitions and working as a commissioned salesperson for a collection agency. He was bigger and stronger than ever in his life and he felt on top of the world. Then he went to his doctor for a routine physical examination. The doc told him his blood pressure was very high and he was taking in enough protein to kill a horse. With his family history of heart trouble, he was advised to seriously consider altering his life style.

As he lay in bed that night, staring at his weight lifting trophies, he couldn't help but lament whether the sacrifice was worth a possible heart attack. His competitive fires were still burning so he decided to compromise by stopping the weight lifting, and after fourteen years, returning to sprinting.

His first few attempts at sprinting were almost his last. Pulled muscles and lack of conditioning and flexibility were obstacles that slowed him down to a crawl. He was astonished that when he did complete a full 100-yard dash without breaking down, his time was nearly equal to his high school time. He had matured, was stronger and had the potential to be faster. He surmised that if he were to be successful, he would have to engage in a proper sprinting program and start all over from scratch. He decided to call on his old high school coach and get his advice When he presented his idea, the coach looked at him with amusement and stated, "You are too old for the sprints. Why don't you try the mile?"

That was all Gary needed to hear. The challenge was on. In high school, the coach was also dubious of Gary's talent. Then he was a skinny introverted young teenager, now he was a confident man, high in self-esteem and physi-

15

cally strong. He would show the coach and anyone else who got in his way.

Gary proceeded to coach himself, reading about running, flexibility, proper nutrition, and creating a goal oriented program. It was at this point that he took a night auditor position at the same Best Western Motel where he had worked before so he could concentrate during the day on his new sport.

Similar to his weightlifting, he started entering competitions and was getting faster and faster. Soon he exceeded his high school times and the local newspapers were covering the track meets to see for themselves if an over thirty year old man could really beat the area's best high school and college sprinters.

Everything was going as Gary had planned, and with regional and national championship medals hanging on his walls, his aspirations of becoming a track coach seemed to be within reach. He was at his athletic peak. Nothing could stop him now.

In the early morning hours of August 13, 1981, he was at his job as the night auditor behind the counter of the Best Western Motel in Albany, New York. Everything would change. He would be stopped almost dead in his tracks. He would be shot and left powerless; another crime victim whose life would never be the same again.

CHAPTER THREE

THE PERPETRATORS

There were six people involved in the robbery of the Best Western Motel in Albany, New York, on August 13, 1981. The victim only saw four of them so the police counted only four. Years later, the true facts would come out. The best way to describe the perpetrators is to give them titles. They are the Three Juveniles, the Wheel Man, the Boss Man and the Shooter.

THE THREE JUVENILES

There is little known about the three juveniles. They were not arrested for this crime although one of them was identified by Goldie Jackson, the Boss Man. His name was Kurt Hall, known on the street as "Can Do". Because he was a juvenile, he may have been referred to Family Court. His record would then have been sealed. The other two young people were known by the street names" Z-Rock" and "Born Justice". Can Do was the one who hopped out of the station wagon to solicit the two more experienced robbers to join them in their caper. He was also the one who had cased the Best Western Motel and discovered the safe in the inner office. During the robbery, he went to the liquor bar side in the motel and watched that door. He emptied the cash register and ripped Gary Geiger's pocket to take his billfold. Born Justice went to the garage side and watched that entrance. Z- Rock was the lookout at the main door of the motel. He never entered the place but watched in the doorway to warn them of an approaching police car or patron.

All three juveniles went to the Falcons Nest, a dance hall and hang out in Albany, the day after the robbery. They were bragging to their homeboys that they had been involved in a robbery and someone had been shot. The code of silence on the streets never blew their cover. They were never caught or charged for the robbery. The word is that they all were involved in other crimes over the years and were incarcerated in New York juvenile and adult correctional facilities. They are now out in the communities and are seen periodically by their old partners in crime.

THE WHEEL MAN

The driver of the car was Ray A. Eaddy. He was born October 8, 1959, and was twenty-one at the time of the crime. After driving his mother's car home and parking it, he had Wayne Blanchard and Goldie Jackson come into the basement of his house and change clothes before sending them out onto the streets of Albany. Ray, who now goes by the name of Ramel, had just completed a two-year hitch with the Marines. He received a good conduct medal and had only been home for twenty-five days. He was out drinking and smoking dope with his friends, and had reluctantly gone along with the idea of robbing the motel. The promise of big money was too appealing to pass up. He had access to his mother's green Chevy wagon and under the influence of smoke dope and alcohol, his judgment was flawed. He would pay dearly for his poor choices. Ramel's version of the robbery had him getting his gun and giving it to the leader of the pack, Goldie Jackson. Goldie gave instructions that a diversionary tactic would be used to distract the motel clerk. Two of their group would fake a fight in the lobby and Goldie would hop over the counter and get the cash. Goldie gave explicit instructions that whoever was in the motel was not to be hurt. Ramel also admonished everyone that no one better be injured. Ramel's account of the robbery was based on his view from inside his vehicle. He was waiting for his accomplices when he heard a shot being fired. Everyone came running out of the motel and jumped into the getaway car. Ramel asked nervously what had happened and was told that Wayne had shot someone. There was an overwhelming state of panic. Ramel observed that "these tough guys now acted like little scared boys, just worrying about themselves."

Ramel did not drive off immediately, much to the dismay of the others. He was composed, and being literally in the driver's seat, he then took over. He heard the sirens in the background and ordered the three juveniles to lie down in the back seat and Goldie and Wayne to sit up front with him. He then proceeded to drive slowly away from the motel in the direction of his own house. On the way, he warned everyone that the individual who had been shot had better not die or they would all be spending the rest of their lives in prison. He asked Wayne why he fired the shot and Wayne mumbled that he had panicked and just wanted everyone to get away. Goldie, at this time, pleaded with Ramel to speed up the car. He said he could run faster than Ramel was traveling. Ramel admonished them that going fast would draw attention to them and that would be the worst thing he could do. When they finally arrived at Ramel's house, he took them into his basement and gave everyone a fresh change of clothes and told them to split up. Before they departed, the money was divided and each got six dollars. Ramel wondered who was holding out. They didn't get much from the robbery, but six dollars apiece was ridiculous. (Wayne and Goldie claimed $150 was the take.)

Ramel later commented that he appeared to be the only one really worried about the victim. He watched television and listened to the radio as the robbery was the top story in Albany for days. He was concerned when he heard that Wayne was playing the big mobster in the streets, bragging about the robbery and how he had shot the clerk. Wayne wanted to enhance his "rep" (reputation) with his peers. Ramel confronted Wayne and told him that if the victim dies "we all go down for murder". At that time in New York, a murder sentence was twenty-five years to life. Today, New York has a death penalty but no one has been executed to date. He told Wayne he would be wise to leave town immediately if not sooner.

Meanwhile, the police were questioning their informants in the streets and the word came down that Goldie had been arrested. He had been identified from a photo line-up by the victim, Gary Geiger. Goldie, thinking if he cooperated he could get a lighter sentence, gave a statement that implicated Wayne Blanchard, Kurt Hall (Can Do) and Ramel Eaddy. After thinking it over, Goldie decided to refuse to sign the statement. Ramel was approached at his place of work by detectives and asked to come down to police headquarters " to answer a few questions". He was shown Goldie's statement but Ramel saw that it was not accurate. Ramel knew he was implicated and the handwriting was on the wall, so he decided to plead guilty and take responsibility for his role in the crime. The district attorney's office allowed Ramel to plead to robbery in the third degree. Ramel was asked to testify at the future trials of Goldie and Wayne. Later on the stand, however, he would take the Fifth Amendment and refuse to testify against Goldie on the grounds that it would incriminate him. He wasn't so worried about doing more time as being labeled a "snitch" and possibly killed in prison or later on the streets. Goldie and Wayne, however, put the word out through the grapevine that Ramel Eaddy was a stool pigeon and he should be taken care of by the brothers. Ramel refused to go into protective custody while in prison, and he had to defend himself several times from potential victimizers. He would end up serving six years and four months in the New York Correctional Facilities in Clinton, Downstate, Ossining (Sing Sing) and Otisville, medium security.

THE BOSS MAN

The Boss Man was known as Goldie Jackson. His actual name was Jay Dee Walker. He was born May 2,1959. He was twenty-two years old at the time of the crime. Being on parole for a previous robbery, he was seeing his parole officer when the Albany police received a call from Parole Officer Holloway that Goldie Jackson was in his office if they wished to question him. Gary Geiger had picked Goldie out of the mug shots so parole was notified that the police saw Goldie as a suspect in the shooting. The following is the police report taken at that time.

Albany Police Department
Continuation/supplemental Report

Day-Date-Time of Incident   2.Date-Time This Report
Th 8-13-81 2:45 AM   8-26-81 6:00 PM

At about 3:14 PM, 8-26-81 the undersigned was informed by the desk officer that Parole Officer Holloway, of the NYS Parole Division called and that he was currently speaking to one Goldie Jackson,APD#01441, who is considered a suspect in the above robbery 1st (shooting).

The undersigned responded along with Det's Galante & Kenyon. We were met by Parole Off. Holloway who directed us to one Goldie JACKSON. We asked JACKSON if we could speak with him and he replied "yes". JACKSON was then read his rights at 3:35 PM, by Det.

John Greene, with Det's Galante, Kenyon, Parole Officers Holloway and Zakon also present. He was then interviewed by the undersigned. At about 3:45 PM, 8-26-81, while in the interview room of the Parole Office, JACKSON orally admitted to the arresting officers that he did act as a look out at the Best Western Motel on Broadway. More specifically he stated that at about 1:30 AM, he went to the Falcon's Nest and met Wayne BLANCHARD, and another guy named KINDU, and Ramel. A fight broke out in front and they decided to leave. He further stated that there were two other black males who he didn't know. They all went behind the Falcon's Nest, got into a green station wagon, NFD. JACKSON got into the passenger seat, Ramel was driving, BLANCHARD was sitting behind RAMEL in the rear seat. KINDU was sitting behind me. The other two young boys were in the far back of the station wagon. They pulled away and started to drive around the City. They were all bull shitting, and someone suggested that they go down to the Best Western Motel, to get some money. They then went down there, it was now about 2:30 AM, when they arrived at the motel. He then stated that Ramel parked the car right in front of the motel, and everybody got out of the car but Ramel. JACKSON then said that he stayed outside the lobby door, and acted as a look out. His job was to summon the other guys if the cops come or anyone else. JACKSON THEN(sic) said that BLANCHARD, KINDU, and the other two young boys then entered the motel. JACKSON then said he stayed outside the lobby door, and a couple of minutes passed. He then said he heard a gun shot and four of the guys came running out. They all got into the car and RAMEL drove away. He then said they dropped him off in the Arbor Hill area. He said that when BLANCHARD got into the car he had a roll of bills with a band around it, like you see in a bank. All of the other young guys were saying that BLANCHARD shot the motel clerk. BLANCHARD was the one who shot the clerk with a silver 22. Cal. Pistol, JACKSON said. The undersigned then asked him to accompany them to the detective office and give them a sworn statement which he complied. Once at the detective office a sworn statement was started by the undersigned with Det. Cunningham present along with Parole Off. Holloway. A short while after it was started JACKSON said he wanted to stop the statement. He was booked for Robbery 1st, while at the detective office, and lodged in the cell block. It should be noted that a photo line up was shown to JACKSON, and he picked out APD#01321, as Wayne BLANCHARD and also APD#53102, as Kindu, identified as

Kurt HALL, as both being involved in the robbery of the Best Western. The five other subjects involved in this incident are still at large at the time of this report.

Det. John Greene

APPROVED

Goldie Jackson was put in the Albany County Detention Facility, better known as the jail. He had been picked out of a set of photos by the victim, Gary Geiger. Goldie was to later say that there was so little taken in the robbery that he refused his share. Goldie then waited in jail until his trial

THE SHOOTER

Wayne Blanchard pulled the trigger in the shooting of the motel clerk on August 13, 1981. Wayne had been out on parole for only four months, having served time for another robbery. His previous crime had been the robbery of a pizza deliveryman in Syracuse, New York. He had pistol-whipped that victim in order to take a few dollars to buy liquor and weed.

Wayne Blanchard was born July 26, 1960, in Albany, New York. He is the tenth of fifteen children. He was seven years old when his father passed away. He was well known at the juvenile detention facility in Albany, being a constant resident there as he grew up. His delinquent behavior included snatching pocket books, shoplifting and strong-armed robbery in the streets. He never used a weapon, just physical intimidation. He stole cars for the joy ride and burglarized homes and "tipped the till" in stores. He smoked cigarettes at age ten and marijuana at twelve. He first smoked grass at Willie and Junior Campbell's house. Wayne stated in an interview with the author that they are both dead now. He was sent to Samanatha Shelter and

Vanderhecten Hall in neighboring Troy, New York. He ran away from both facilities.

In ninth grade, he was kicked out of high school the very first day. He transferred to School 24, a Magnet school in Albany. For his continued juvenile delinquency behavior, the Family Court finally sent him to Highland Training School and later to the Industry Training School. When he was sixteen, he was at a movie with the other Industry Training School participants and stopped at another resident's house in Syracuse. They called for a pizza to be delivered at an apartment building nearby. When the delivery person came into the stairwell, Wayne and three of his partners in crime asked him for change and then took his wallet and watch, beat him up and then ran. They went to hide in their friend's apartment. The deliveryman was Greek and his billfold had mostly Greek money. They were apprehended, and Wayne spent seven months in the Onondaga County jail. He was returned to the Industrial Training School and given five years probation. On his second pass home for a visit, Wayne decided not to go back. He proceeded to snatch another purse and was caught. He was sentenced to two and a third years in the New York State correctional system. Wayne Blanchard had graduated to the big time.

It was now May of 1977 and Wayne would do the two and a third years and an additional six months prison time. He violated his parole after only being out for one month. He was in the Albany County Jail for sixty days and then sent back to the state correctional system for one year. He was out for only four months on parole again when the Best Western robbery took place. It was August 13, 1981.

Wayne Blanchard's version of the holdup was slightly different from the other participants. He said he and Goldie Jackson were at Arthur's Round Table, a bar on Northern Boulevard and Second Avenue in Albany, New York. They were drinking and smoking weed when Ramel pulled up in a station wagon. Can Do hopped out and said he knew where to get $50,000 in a safe in a hotel. Goldie at first said no because he wondered why they wanted to include more people in on the score. Wayne did not hesitate and went right to his crib and got his gun. He had stolen the gun from the car of a drug dealer. He thought he was taking dope when he picked up a brown bag from the front seat of the car. It was a gun. Goldie also had a gun. Can Do knew the layout because he had cased the hotel. The plan was to have Goldie and Wayne go to the desk and ask about room rates. Can Do went to the bar side and Born Justice to the garage entrance. Z Rock would be the look out and Ramel would stay by the car. After entering the lobby and approaching the clerk, Goldie jumped over the counter and said, "This is a stick up." Wayne went around the corner and discovered the safe in the back office. Goldie backed Gary Geiger into the office. Gary told them he did not know the combination. Meanwhile, Can Do emptied the cash register. Goldie hit Gary with the gun but Gary keep insisting that he did not know the combination. They finally believed him when he said the manager was the only one who had the combination and he was sleeping upstairs in one of the rooms. They decided to blow this "pop stand". It turned out to produce only "chump change". They ran out to the waiting car. Wayne took one more look in to see if the clerk was still knocked out. He saw the clerk getting up and running to what he thought was a box on the wall. He hollered at him, took one shot and ran out.

They went to Ramel's mother's house to split up the money. Their total take, according to Wayne, was one hundred and fifty dollars. Goldie and Wayne left Ramel's house and started walking down the street. Z Rock, Ramel, Can Do and Born Justice went to the Falcon's Nest, a local dance hall. Wayne went back to his house to put his gun up and then he also went to the Falcon's Nest. People were already talking about the robbery. Wayne knew he had to leave town.

Leaving the Falcon's Nest at 3:30 a.m., Wayne was walking down the street when he was picked up by the Albany police. He had changed clothes. They questioned him on the sidewalk and he told them he had been at the Falcon's Nest from 11:00 p.m. on. He told them he was on parole and was not going to get into any trouble. They let him go. He went to his house on Second Street and listened to the news on the radio. The clerk was in stable but guarded condition. Wayne went to Goldie's place on Clinton Avenue. Goldie had also heard the latest news so they decided they had better " book it" and leave town. They went around looking for some one to give them money to finance their trip. They hid out at another friend's house. Wayne had reported to his parole officer the day of the robbery so he thought his parole officer would not suspect him of any wrong doing. He would not have to report in for another month.

Wayne sold his gun to Ramel to get some money. Goldie and Wayne went to the Schenectady bus station. They didn't think the Albany bus station was safe as it was right next to the scene of the crime. They took the Greyhound bus to the Port Authority in New York City. Wayne and Goldie went to the Bronx to an old girlfriend's house. Then they both took the Amtrak train to Philadelphia. Wayne had an uncle there and they could crash with him for a while. Goldie stayed with Wayne for two weeks. One morning Wayne got up and Goldie was gone.

Wayne later called an old girl friend in Albany to see what was going down about the robbery. She told him Goldie had been arrested at his parole officer's office. She said that when they told Goldie he was under arrest for the robbery and shooting, he tried to run and was tackled by the parole officer.

Wayne called his sister, Josephine, to get more money. He then took a bus to Tupelo, Mississippi. He stayed at his brother Bobby's pad. Wayne worked cleaning parking lots hosing them down. He would steal food and clothes. He robbed homosexuals and used their checks to buy expensive items and then turn the merchandise back in with the receipts to get cash. Wayne's cousin, Earl Blanchard, was one of his relatives he hung out with in Tupelo. Earl was a car thief (Wayne's words), and he and Wayne would joyride all over Mississippi. Wayne was getting high on tequila and Tanqueray gin on the rocks. Wayne then stayed with a woman called Barbara, but his life- style soon had upset her and she threw him out. He had gotten into a fight earlier with Barbara's brother over weed and that was the last straw. Wayne and his cousin Earl then stole money from their uncle, a truck driver, while he was out on the road. Wayne and another cousin, James McGrady, stole a Ford Thunderbird and drove up to Illinois. James stopped for gas while Wayne was sleeping and pulled away from the station without paying for the gas. It was now December 22, 1981, four months since the robbery and shooting. The Illinois Highway Patrol pulled them over near Peoria. James insisted that he had paid but the trooper doubled checked with the station and the woman attendant said they did not and she wanted them arrested. Wayne identified himself as Bobby Blanchard, using his brother's name. Wayne's luck was running out. Bobby Blanchard was also wanted on an outstanding warrant. Wayne and James were both arrested and their fingerprints were taken. Wayne was identified as wanted on the robbery and shooting in New York. His parole agent came to Peoria to bring him back to Albany. Wayne contemplated running while he was being transported by airplane. They did not use handcuffs on the plane. He thought it over but decided that he would look guilty if he did. He seriously pondered the idea that he could still beat the rap. The clerk would never be able to identify him with all the confusion of the robbery. Besides, with four Black faces, a white dude would never be able to tell them apart. Didn't they say that all Black people looked alike to them? He was surprised to be arraigned and charged with robbery in the first degree and aggravated assault with a deadly weapon. He was put in the Albany County Jail with no bail. He talked to Goldie Jackson, his partner in crime, every day. Goldie's trial was now in progress.

CHAPTER FOUR

THE TRIALS

New York has a State Unified Court System. There are four judicial departments and twelve judicial districts in the entire state. The appellate courts are made up of the Court of Appeals, Appellate Divisions of the Supreme Court and Appellate Terms of the Supreme Court. Next are the trial courts, which are statewide and include the Supreme Court, Court of Claims, Family Court and Surrogate's Court. In New York City there are Criminal Court and Civil Court. Outside New York City there are County Court, City Courts, Town and Village Courts and District Courts. The state of New York is also unique in that it has available in every county, community dispute resolution centers to handle selected felonies, civil and misdemeanor criminal matters and appropriate Family Court cases. They offer to victims of crime the opportunity to meet their offender in a dialogue mediation to help bring information and closure to a traumatic situation. Gary Geiger made good use of this resource.

The County Court in Albany, New York, Third Judicial Department, Third Judicial District, had jurisdiction over the trials of the suspects in the robbery and assault at the Best Western Motel on August 13, 1981. The Honorable John J. Clyne was selected as the presiding judge for the case against Goldie Jackson, also known as (a.k.a.) Jay Dee Walker. Albany County citizens had elected the Honorable

Sol Greenberg as their district attorney. He assigned his assistant, Christopher Rutnik, as the prosecutor for this case. Goldie Jackson's lawyer was Stanley Segal, a noted criminal attorney. Goldie Jackson's trial was fairly cut and dried. The police testified about his statements to them, and although Goldie refused to sign his confession and later recanted any involvement, he was implicated by his own words. The key witness was the very victim, Gary Geiger. Although Gary initially only could say he was robbed by four men who were Black and about 5 feet 7 inches tall, he did say one was between 170 and 190 pounds and was "very muscular". The others were smaller and around 140 pounds. They all were wearing jeans and sneakers and had close-cropped hair. In first seeing a photo line up, he wasn't sure about his identification of Goldie Jackson, Wayne Blanchard and Kurt Hall. They were possible assailants. Only later when he had nightmares about the shooting did he see the faces again. Every night he relived the trauma as if it was happening all over again. Now he could see the faces clearly. He called Detective Greene and asked to see the eleven photos again, and this time he picked out Goldie Jackson.

In the court room, prosecutor Christopher Rutnik gave an opening statement saying evidence would show that Jackson was present during the robbery and either was the "muscle man" described by Geiger or a lookout as he admitted in his statement given to the police. Geiger was the first witness to be called. He gave a graphic and emotional account of his ordeal, and he identified Jackson as the man who wore a tanktop and baseball cap during the robbery. Gary Geiger's own weightlifting experience came into play. In his identification of Jackson, Geiger said to the jury, "Weight lifting is not my hobby, it's my life. He (Jackson) had a good set of shoulder muscles, but not overly large. I wondered if this man worked out." He said he made a mental note of the perpetrators physical appearances. He then proceeded to walk down to the defendant's table and stood face to face in front of Goldie Jackson. Accuser and the accused. Mano e mano. Jackson was asked by the prosecutor to take off his suit coat. Jackson was over six feet tall and his broad chest and heavily muscled arms were readily apparent. (His last bit in prison lifting weights now contributed to his downfall. Jackson would later say he should never have agreed to take off his suit coat.) Gary Geiger studied him carefully and then announced, "Yes, he is the man." Ray A. Eaddy decided not to testify at Goldie's trial and he took the Fifth Amendment stating he would not answer any questions on the grounds it would incriminate him. The jury came back quickly with a guilty verdict. Judge John A. Clyne, who had the reputation of a "hanging judge," had no hesitation and sentenced Goldie Jackson to twelve and one half to twenty-five years in the New York State prison system.

It was then Wayne Blanchard's turn to face the music. Wayne was put in a lineup at the county jail. Wayne called his brother, Fields, to participate in the lineup in an effort to confuse Gary Geiger. Wayne was sitting in a room waiting for the lineup when Gary Geiger came by the open door that had a window in it. Wayne's attorney, Elena Vaida, would later state that the line-up was tainted because Gary Geiger could have seen Wayne Blanchard in the room before the line-up. Judge Joseph Harris, also a no-nonsense judge, overruled the objection. Gary Geiger, fresh from his nightmare dreams, had no trouble picking out Wayne Blanchard as one of his assailants. The prosecution offered ten to twenty years as a plea bargain.

Wayne Blanchard said he would take a seven and one half to fifteen or an eight and one half to twenty-five, but there was no way he would take a deal on a double digit sentence. Wayne Blanchard was willing to take his chances at a trial. His lawyer who was just out of the factory (law school) decided that the fact that Gary Geiger saw Wayne in his dreams could be challenged and beaten in the courtroom. In turn, the district attorney's office was not willing to offer a lower plea bargain because they already had a conviction on Goldie Jackson and with Gary Geiger as the victim and eye witness, they were confident of a conviction and being able to put away a trouble maker like Wayne Blanchard for a long time.

The trial witnesses consisted of the motel owner, the hotel manager, Ray A. Eaddy and the key witness, Gary Geiger. Ray A. Eaddy was offered a one to three year sentence to testify against Wayne. With Goldie Jackson already convicted, Ray A. Eaddy thought there would be no harm if he testified. Wayne, he thought, was going to be convicted anyway. He might just as well get the best deal he could. It was now a case of every man for himself. For a reduced sentenced promised by the district attorney's office, he decided that this time he would cooperate. On the stand, Ray A Eaddy reluctantly testified that Wayne told him, "I shot the dude." Wayne Blanchard's parole officer also testified that Wayne was in to see him the day of the robbery and then promptly left town. He needed to have permission to leave Albany. It did not look good for Wayne Blanchard. Wayne decided not to testify because he would have trouble explaining why he ran after the crime if he was not involved. Wayne's attorney had a lot of enthusiasm. Not only was she a brand new attorney but this was her first big case. She, too, was a minority, and she liked Wayne. She said she enjoyed representing him because he was a gentleman all the way. He had a tough life and she would do her best in defending him. The State would have to prove him guilty beyond a shadow of a doubt before they could convict him. She became very aggressive when she cross examined Gary Geiger. He had testified that he recognized Wayne Blanchard in his dreams four months after the robbery. She accused Gary of being influenced or "steered" by the police, and that he really could not have recognized Wayne Blanchard unless the police told him " this is your man". She ridiculed his identification and said no jury in the world would convict a person on a vague dream that long after the crime. She accused Gary Geiger of enjoying being the center of attention with all the press and television coverage. After all, he was a known weightlifter and champion sprinter, and there he was, in the limelight again. Gary Geiger was getting angry on the stand just as the defense attorney had hoped. He said he did not "enjoy" getting shot and left to die. But Elena Vaida was beginning to create some doubt in the minds of the jurors. She could sense it. All she needed, they told her in law school, was one juror who wasn't sure. Gary Geiger would later comment that he felt more victimized by the defense attorney than he did getting shot. He didn't know he was shot right away but he was sure he was being revictimized by this eager and, he thought, overzealous attorney. She was just doing her job but she was also doing a number on the victim. But Gary Geiger again calmly walked down from the witness chair and stood in front of Wayne Blanchard and said this was the man who robbed and shot him. Wayne Blanchard did not look at Gary Geiger, and this would stick in Gary's mind. This tough guy who had shot him was not man enough to even look him in the eye. The case was now in the jury's hands.

The jury must have thought the dream sequence was difficult to swallow also. The identification was the crucial issue since the testimony indicated Geiger did not give a positive identification of Blanchard's photo shortly after the robbery and said he based his eventual identification upon vivid dreams which became clear four months later. The six woman and six man jury came in at 4:45 p.m. and said they were " hopelessly deadlocked" as they had been twenty four hours earlier. They had deliberated for two days, and three times they came back to Judge Harris and said they were still without a verdict. One juror had his hat and coat on after the third deadlock announcement. Judge Harris gruffly said, "Where do you think you are going? You are staying here until you come up with a verdict!" The jury went back into the jurors' room, and finally, at 9:30 p.m., reached a verdict. Guilty on all counts. Wayne Blanchard, although disappointed in the verdict, was actually glad when the trial was all over. He thought the whole trial scene was like a circus. People and witnesses were paraded in and the district attorney, judge and even his own attorney contributed to the three ring affair. Gary Geiger also thought the entire process was demeaning and degrading. It was interesting to hear the same opinion coming from the victim and the perpetrator. The system had victimized them both.

Wayne Blanchard now figured he was still young at twenty-one, almost twenty-two. When he was sentenced to twelve and one half to twenty-five years in the state penitentiary, he figured he would be thirty-three when he got out and would still have the major part of his life in front of him. His other prison experience had been a waste of time. He shot basketball and lifted weights and bragged about all the "bad" things he had done. His focus was on earning a tough reputation among his homeboys and not rehabilitation. This time, he told himself, he would grow up and apply himself. He was tired of being on the run and going nowhere with his life. It would be different this time around. He would get his high school graduate equivalency degree (GED) and learn a trade.

On June 15, 1982, at 10 a.m., Wayne Blanchard was sentenced to twelve and one half to twenty-five years in prison by Judge Joseph Harris. He would serve his time in

Clinton, Danamora, Downstate Correctional Facility, Comstock, Great Meadow, and then Eastern Correctional Facility. It would be in Eastern Correctional Facility in Ellenville, New York, that Wayne Blanchard and Gary Geiger would meet again ten years later.

Ray A.Eaddy, Goldie Jackson and Wayne Blanchard were in prison, taking the consequences for their crime. Gary Geiger could now go on with his life. His fears were behind him. He had overcome a robbery, a shooting and the burden of two trials and the slow, methodical criminal justice system. Or, that is what everybody told him. But it wouldn't be that easy. Post-traumatic stress would rear its ugly head and Gary Geiger's nightmares would go on and on and on.

CHAPTER FIVE

POST-TRAUMATIC STRESS

Post-traumatic stress disorder (PTSD) is a form of anxiety disorder triggered by memories of a traumatic event — an event that directly affected the person or one that the individual witnessed. The disorder commonly affects survivors of traumatic events such as sexual assault, physical assault (Gary Geiger's being shot), war, torture, natural disasters, automobile accidents, airplane crashes, hostage situations or a death camp. The affliction can also affect rescue workers at an airplane crash (September 11, 2001) or a mass shooting or witnesses or survivors of a tragic accident. Not everyone involved in a post-traumatic stress disorder event experiences post-traumatic stress disorder. But post-traumatic stress disorder may affect about one in twenty-five adults in the United States. Thirteen million Americans suffer from post-traumatic stress. The disorder affects men and women in about the same numbers. Treatment may involve a combined approach including medications and behavior therapies designed to help the person gain control of her or his anxiety.

The brain cells tell of the danger. Childhood experiences can affect a person's reaction to a traumatic event. For example, a family history of anxiety, alcohol abuse or being part of a dysfunctional family can be a determining factor. One can have nightmares and flashbacks and certain events can trigger post-traumatic stress. There is also survivor guilt.

Symptoms include distress on anniversaries of the trauma, efforts to avoid thoughts, feelings and activities associated with the trauma and feelings of detachment or estrangement from others with an inability to have love feelings. There can also be a marked, diminished interest or participation in activities that once were an important source of enjoyment. An individual can have a sense of hopelessness about the future—no hope of a family life, career or living to an old age. A person can have trouble sleeping, become angry easily and have trouble concentrating. Victims can experience an exaggerated startle response to noise. Physiologic reactions may include an increase in blood pressure, rapid heart rate, fast breathing, muscle tension, nausea and diarrhea. PTSD is experienced by at least 60% of victims of violent crime with many experiencing symptoms for a few months; however, many victims will suffer and experience PTSD for many years, affecting their lives in several ways. The classic symptoms of PTSD are: anger, depression, guilt, denial and fear. (The majority of this information is taken from the Mayo Clinic. com web site, personal research and the 2002 public television program on The Brain).

After the trial and sentencing, Gary Geiger was out of work and at one point staying at the Y.M.C.A. As previously stated, he reached in his pocket one day and had only twenty-five cents to his name. He knew he needed counseling to cope with his condition, but he didn't have insurance and no counselor would see him as a patient. He began to suffer from post-traumatic stress disorder. He had many of the symptoms described above. Not only did he continue to have very real nightmares and flashbacks, but he began to watch his rearview mirror, looking for friends of Goldie and Wayne to come after him. He would have feelings of road rage if someone cut him off. He often would pull his car over at the side of the road and try to calm down. Not able to return to the motel, he found what work he could, and in the fall of 1982, he landed a job at the New York State Office of Mental Retardation and Developmental Disabilities (OMRDD) as an account clerk. At work, he was jumpy and would bark back at fellow employees, and even his supervisors when they would come up behind him or criticize his work or his manner. His dysfunctional family history with alcohol abuse, coupled with the shooting and trial set him up to be a prime candidate for post-traumatic stress disorder. He became a loner, and his relationships with women were limited. His supervisor recommended that he get treatment. In Gary Geiger's own words, he provides a synopsis of his experience with PTSD and how he finally came to the final stage of acceptance. "Subsequent to the trials and convictions of Wayne Blanchard and Goldie Jackson and their respective sentences, one would think that I should have been elated, the good guys won, the bad guys were going to state prison for a long time, justice was served, the system worked, but at whose expense? I remember exiting the courtroom after the Blanchard trial a very confused, angry man who had lost his identity and felt used and re-victimized by the justice system. Instead of being involved with the trial and having a say, I felt like a mere piece of evidence, merely a witness. I wanted to be part of the proceedings, have an opportunity to relate what this incident did to my life and all those people near to me. I could only speak about what I had witnessed, not what I was feeling or going through. After all, I was told, the case was the State of New York vs. the Offenders. No mention was given to my name. I didn't even have anyone to represent me. Something felt adversarial; it seemed like us against them, confrontational."

"The anger I felt would manifest itself in many ways in the ensuing months and years. Living in virtual squalor subsequent to being fired by the motel, I was enticed every day by my neighbors to partake of alcohol and/or drugs to escape and alleviate the pain I was experiencing from not only the incident but the trials as well. I rejected that route, but the anger had to go somewhere, the frustration has to come out somehow, and it did in many insidious ways. Of all the stages of PTSD, anger at the offenders, anger at the system, anger at everyone, I was an accident waiting to happen, and didn't know how to escape this box I was living in."

"A year after the incident, I started to work for the State of New York in a job beneath my capabilities, an entry-level job but a job nonetheless. Part of my job was to ascertain that computer printouts were delivered to the correct stations, that the print on the computer was legible. If not, I had to install a new printer ribbon. One morning only 3 months into the job, my supervisor felt that I had been negligent in my duties and approached me in a very confrontational and aggressive manner. In an instant, I flashed back to a year previous when Wayne Blanchard approached me with his silver plated revolver. Without touching my supervisor, I backed him into a corner and admonished him to never approach me again in this manner and if he did there would be repercussions. The Personnel Department did not buy my explanation of what happened and consequently I was transferred to another agency where I bumped a part-time employee who was well liked. Very little was known at the time regarding PTSD and I was labeled a 'problem' and cast off to someone else."

"We hear so much today about road rage and misplaced anger out on the highways, which has led to many confrontations and deaths as well. I was practicing road rage in the early and mid eighties whenever a motorist would improperly signal, cut me off, or tail gate me. My usual approach would be to follow the individual until he pulled up to a stoplight where upon I would exit my car and create a scene, screaming and yelling at the driver at how inept they were.

Ultimately, cars would line up behind me and yell and honk their horns until I came to my senses and drove off. In one particular incident the situation escalated and I pulled the driver through the window, an assault case for sure if he wanted to press charges. I was slowly evolving from the victim to the victimizer and I didn't know why. The only solace I could find was in my running and weight lifting workouts, and even there I was not as proficient in them as I was before the incident."

"After a series of shouting incidents at work, I volunteered myself to Employee Health Services for counseling in the late eighties. I was being counseled by an expert in PTSD and learned that I was diagnosed with it, a severe case to be sure. I attended several sessions and talking about it seemed to help, but there was one thing the counselor could not do, and that was, answer the questions that had been bothering me for so long. Subsequent to my mediation with Wayne Blanchard and several conversations regarding conflict resolution with Tom Christian (the author), my interpersonal relationships improved dramatically as well as the way I handled everyday conflict in my life. The hundreds of speeches that I have given over the past decade have also improved my self-esteem. My PTSD rears its head every so often. It's something I'm told that will never completely go away. I still have problems at times, with people, but as Tom Christian always said, "It is their problem until you make it yours." That remark has stayed with me whenever I feel like slipping back to the old way I reacted to stress. There is so much more help available today, and if I had a serious problem again with PTSD, I would seek counseling. This is something I stress to every victim's group that I have addressed. Seek help. Do not underestimate the emotional damage that being a victim can have."

CHAPTER SIX

THE MEDIATION

The years went by but the problems continued. Gary Geiger's life was unsettled and he suffered from lack of closure. His family and friends told him to put it behind him and go on with his life. It was easy to say, but Gary couldn't seem to get over the tragedy that he had experienced. In 1991, Gary was watching television one night and a special program on Home Box Office (HBO) caught his attention. It was called <u>Confrontation</u>. In the program, a New York City teacher, Gary Smith, had been savagely beaten with a baseball bat and was left to die. Another teacher performed a tracheotomy on him and he was rushed to the hospital. He was in a coma for days and six operations were performed on him before he could be released from the medical facility. Gary Smith had been a teacher in the Bronx, New York City, for seventeen years. He loved his job and the kids respected him. He was a dedicated person and a valued asset to the school system. Why was he attacked and almost killed? It was a question that Gary Smith could not answer. He had been umpiring a girls' softball tournament for the school physical education program when a young man not associated with the school came up behind the backstop. He began to go through the girls' book bags. Mr. Smith saw him, and in between innings he cautiously approached the young man and asked if he could help him. The young man, in his late teens, said he had picked up a loose softball and thrown it back to the catcher. A large ring he had been wearing flew off when he threw the ball. He was looking for it in the area it had fallen, that is, by the book bags. Mr. Smith looked briefly with him and then had to go back behind the pitcher's mound to continue umpiring the game. He told the young man that he would have to stop picking through the girls' book bags.

No sooner had Mr. Smith returned to the pitcher's mound when he saw the young man pick up an aluminum softball bat and begin to walk away. He made what he thought was a wise decision to not confront the young man and let him take the bat. It was better than causing a scene. The young man, however, went around the school building and soon came back. He laid the aluminum bat down by the players' bench and picked up a wooden bat. He then raced at Mr. Smith and proceeded to pummel him, first on the teacher's arms as he raised them trying to defend himself, and then as his arms fell from the blows, he hit him on his head. With his wrist broken, Gary Smith quickly dropped his hands and received a knockout blow to his head. As he lay on the playground, his attacker continued to hit him mercilessly. The students were screaming, and one ran to the school for help. The commotion stopped the young man, and he dropped the bat and ran. With blood pouring down his face from the head wound, Gary Smith was choking to death from the blood in his throat and a crushed windpipe. Another teacher cut a plastic pen in half and by opening a hole through his neck and inserting the hollow pen, allowed Gary to breathe. The education teacher had learned the technique in first aid class. It saved Gary Smith's life. The ambulance raced through the streets of the Bronx. Another senseless crime of violence was reported on the news that evening, only this time it was a well liked teacher and the community was up in arms.

The young man, Tommy Brown, heard the ambulance

and saw the news on television. He turned himself in, worrying that a vigilante group might hunt him down. He pleaded guilty to assault with a deadly weapon and was sentenced to five to fifteen years in the New York State Correctional Facility at Elmira. Gary Smith, with facial injuries and minus the vision from one eye, was at Tommy Brown's sentencing, sitting in the public area of the courtroom.

One year later, a reporter from the New York Times wrote an article about Gary Smith, asking the question, "Where is he now?" The writer described how Gary had tried to go back to teaching but suffered severe headaches and became dizzy on his feet. With no depth vision, he could not teach gymnastics anymore. He now worked for the teachers' union and helped other teachers who were attacked by students. The article ended with Gary Smith stating," I never knew why the young man attacked me. I loved teaching and young people. This is not over until I can talk to Tommy Brown and ask him why he attacked me."

Gaby Monet, a producer for the Home Box Office television channel, read the New York Times article about Gary Smith and thought the incident would make an exciting and appealing program. She contacted Gary Smith and asked him if he would be interested in traveling to Elmira, New York, and meeting face to face with Tommy Brown in the correctional facility. Although his wife thought he was crazy to meet with the person who almost killed him, Gary Smith was definitely interested. Ms. Monet then called this author's office at the New York State Unified Court System Community Dispute Resolution Centers Program (CDRCP). She wanted to know if the court program conducted mediation in a prison setting between a crime victim and the person who committed the crime. The CDRCP director told her that the program did mediate this type of situation if the victim requested it and the New York State Department of Corrections approved it. This type of program was called Victim and Offender Mediation (VOM). Gaby Monet presented the circumstances of Gary Smith and Tommy Brown. The CDRCP staff told her that the program was voluntary and confidential. To have HBO film it would not be acceptable unless both parties agreed. The CDRCP director also told her that the victim and offender would have to be interviewed to determine if they were appropriate for this process. Then they would have to be prepared for the meeting. The victim would have to want the meeting to get information and closure and not use it to verbally attack the offender. (There is a process before sentencing for a victim to make what is called a victim impact statement. At this time, the victim can relate to the court and the offender what the crime has done to the victim and the family. This is completely a separate process from victim and offender mediation.) In order to consider a possible mediation, the offender would have to admit to the crime and express some type of remorse for his or her behavior. Many times an offender does not want to admit to a crime because he or she may be hoping for an appeal. Based on the information obtained from the victim, Gary Smith, he was considered a good candidate for the process. He wanted information and closure. The VOM program then interviewed Tommy Brown in Elmira Correctional Facility and found out that not only did he take full responsibility for his behavior, he looked forward to talking to Gary Smith and expressing his remorse. They both agreed to have it filmed by HBO so the film could be shown at high schools and other forums to help young people make better choices.

The New York State Court System worked closely with Thomas Coughlin (now deceased), then Commissioner of the New York State Department of Corrections and his Director of Public Information, James Flateau, to provide this service at the request of the victim of a crime. Permission to mediate in a correctional facility was granted.

The mediator for this meeting was Peter Bibby from the Center for Dispute Settlement, Inc. in Rochester, New York. Andrew Thomas is the Executive Director. Both Gary Smith and Tommy Brown were Black so the mediator chosen was also Black. (This is not always necessary but it is usually more effective when dealing with people of the same race. A key component in a mediation is a trust level which has to be developed between the two parties and the mediator. For example, if a victim is a woman and the offender is a man, it is recommended that there be co-mediators, a woman and a man).

Tom Christian flew with Gary Smith from New York City to Elmira and prepared him for the mediation and the prison setting. HBO had their cameras set back so they were only as intrusive as necessary. The mediation went well and Gary Smith received answers to his questions. Tommy Brown told him he had dropped out of school. He had been a basketball star in high school and had felt the pressure to succeed. His parents were going through a divorce and Tommy Brown's answer to his problems was to quit everything. He was on the streets trying to seek comfort from drugs and earn money by selling dope. He was an angry young man and rage was building up in him. He did not attend Gary Smith's school. They did not know each other before the attack. Tommy Brown was upset when Mr. Smith did not help him find his lost ring. Everything exploded inside Tommy Brown. He went off, and Gary Smith was the closest target. All of his frustration and anger were unloaded on Gary Smith, the teacher and symbol of authority. In the mediation, Tommy Brown apologized for his behavior and took full responsibility for his actions. His explanation for his behavior was not an excuse but the way his mind was thinking at the time. In the course of the mediation, Gary Smith accepted the apology from Tommy Brown and forgave him. He encouraged Tommy Brown to get his life together and look to the future. He told him he was young and could go on to a productive life, and he hoped this meeting would help him. After the mediation, Gary Smith said he felt at peace and could go on with his life. The teachers in Elmira Correctional Facility said Tommy Brown was like a different individual after the mediation. It appeared a burden had been lifted off his shoulders. (People who watch the HBO video say they can almost see this happening.) He also applied himself more in his school-work and his attitude changed dramatically for the better. Gaby Monet and the people at HBO were very happy with their program and the New York State Court System had helped another victim and offender find a sense of justice. They also received an excellent new training tape for their statewide mediation programs.

Meanwhile, back in Albany, New York, Gary Geiger was lying on his couch, and by chance, was watching the same HBO Special called <u>Confrontation</u>. He rolled off his couch and said, "That is what I need. I have to talk to the guy who shot me."

He tried to get the phone number of the mediation program from the credits at the end of the program. As happens so often on programs like this, he didn't get the number. He called HBO the next day and they gave him the number of the Community Dispute Resolution Program for the New York State Unified Court System. Tom Christian took his call.

An appointment was set up, and Gary Geiger nervously came to the CDRCP office in Albany, New York. He was met by the smiling face of Yvonne Taylor. Yvonne was an attractive Black woman who had worked for the state for over twenty years. She was not "burned out" nor did she give the appearance that you were bothering her, but to the contrary, she had the unique talent of making a person feel that she had been waiting for you to come and you were someone special. Gary Geiger felt more comfortable right away. He didn't have to wait because Yvonne ushered him right into the director's office.

This author, Thomas Frank Christian, was the director of the Community Dispute Resolution Centers Program for the New York State Unified Court System. He started the mediation programs for the New York State Court System in 1981, and held the position of State Director until he retired at the end of 1996. His other positions included Director of the Alternatives to Incarceration Project for the National Center for State Courts that served twelve southern states, state director of the Minnesota Community Corrections Association, and director of an award winning community-based correctional program. He had worked in correctional institutions and had been a senior probation officer from Hennepin County Court Services in Minneapolis, Minnesota. In 1979, he was voted the Corrections Professional of the year by the Minnesota Corrections Association. He earned a master's degree in criminal justice and a doctorate in social science from the School of Criminal Justice at Michigan State University. The author will be identified as Tom Christian in the following pages.

Tom Christian also welcomed Gary Geiger and listened to his explanation of why he wanted to meet with Wayne Blanchard. Gary gave all the right reasons for his request. He needed information as to why Wayne Blanchard shot him when he had cooperated in every way he could during the robbery. He wanted to heal from his years of post-traumatic stress. He wanted to see and finally talk to this person who had caused so much disruption in his life. He saw him as a monster. Now, he wanted to meet him as a person. Tom Christian quizzed him on a number of issues to measure Gary's anger and resentment. Tom told Gary that his session was not a time to dump all his built up feelings on Wayne Blanchard. At the end of the first meeting, Tom Christian told Gary to go home and think about his situation and talk to his counselor to see if it was the right time for him to go through this experience. Gary came back for his second meeting with the name of the therapist that he had been working with over the last couple of years. Consulting with the professional therapist, Tom Christian was told that Gary Geiger was at a place in his treatment where he was not only ready but would benefit greatly from a meeting with Wayne Blanchard. It was time to talk to the New York State Department of Corrections.

With a career in the field of criminal justice, Tom Christian had developed a good relationship with the New York Department of Corrections. At several meetings, he had spoken with State Corrections Commissioner Thomas Coughlin. Tom Christian's Minnesota background in corrections served him well. His first contact for these encounters was, again, James Flateau, the Public Information Officer for State Commissioner Thomas Coughlin. James Flateau then contacted the superintendent of the correctional facility where the offender was housed. In the case of Wayne Blanchard, it was Eastern Correctional Facility at Ellenville, New York. Ellenville was about seventy-five miles north of New York City and seventy-five miles south of Albany, New York. The superintendent, William Mitchel, had the reputation as the best warden in the state and he quickly signed off on the visit. Tom Christian's next contact was with Wayne Blanchard's counselor in Eastern Correctional Facility. His counselor was Mark Ackerhalt. With the cooperation of all the parties in the system, the mediation will have a much better chance of being effective. If a counselor does not feel a part of the process, he or she can sabotage the best laid plans. In talking to Mark Ackerhalt, Tom Christian called on his own background in working with offenders over the years and explained to Mr. Ackerhalt how the victim and offender mediation can be beneficial to the victim and the offender and, in some ways, can make the job of the counselor more effective. Mark Ackerhalt had not been involved in this experience so he was initially skeptical. He was aware of the process and he realized the benefit for the victim as long as that person did not use the meeting as a time to scream and confront the offender. He did not think it would help an offender. He thought that most offenders were too ingrained in the prison culture to benefit from the process. Tom explained to him that many times a major, positive intervention in a prisoner's life can be effective. Mark Ackerhalt decided to talk to Wayne Blanchard and see if he was open to an initial meeting with Tom Christian. Tom knew that if he could talk to the offender he could give him enough information that would convince him that it would be helpful to all concerned including the offender. The call came back that Wayne Blanchard would meet with Tom Christian, but he was bewildered by the request. Tom Christian drove down to Eastern Correctional Facility and sat with Mark Ackerhalt to talk about the process of victim and offender mediation and to get his insights into the behavior and attitude of Wayne Blanchard in the institution and his response to being incarcerated now for eleven years. Mark Ackerhalt said Wayne was not a problem in the facility but was just doing his prison term one day at a time. He was leery of Wayne manipulating the situation to his advantage. Wayne did have the reputation of being a tough, street-wise dude who strutted around the institution, giving the impression he should not be messed with or one had better be prepared to suffer the consequences.

Wayne came into the counseling room with a confused look on his face. "Who is this Tom Christian and what trouble is he going to cause for me?" was the non-verbal message he gave. Tom Christian explained who he was and told him a little of his corrections background. Tom also tried to get Wayne to trust him by explaining to him that Tom had an uncle and cousin do time in prison. Tom had people on both sides of the law. Tom's grandfather, William Carney, had been a deputy federal marshal and died from injuries suffered in the line of duty. His father, Edward Christian, and Tom's brother, Kenneth Christian, had been in the law enforcement field for over thirty years each. Tom then described to Wayne the needs of Gary Geiger and how Wayne could help Gary deal with his post-traumatic stress. Wayne was told that only he could give Gary the answers to certain questions. Wayne appeared surprised and said he thought that Gary would have long forgotten about the incident and would have gone on with his life. Tom gave Wayne a short course on victimology and became impressed with Wayne's concern and interest in helping Gary. The two key questions now had to be asked. First, did Wayne admit to being the shooter and, secondly, was there any remorse for his actions? Wayne was very forthcoming and quickly took responsibility as the trigger-man. He also stated that he was sorry for all the pain and suffering he had caused Gary and his family. He had fired the gun at the spur of the moment when he thought Gary was running towards an alarm, and now wished he had just" booked it" out of that motel. Tom was convinced of Wayne's sincerity and told him that he would serve as the mediator in their encounter, and that he would now talk to Wayne's counselor, Mr. Ackerhalt, and then go back to Albany and prepare Gary for a possible meeting with Wayne. Tom assured Wayne that he would not allow the mediation to become an opportunity for Gary to scream and berate Wayne for what he had done to him. If there was a chance of this happening, he said he would not have approved the meeting. Tom asked Wayne if he trusted him to help him as well as Gary Geiger to benefit from the mediation. Wayne said he did. Wayne was happy, and in his own way, relieved. Tom told him that if and when there was a mediation, he would send a letter to be placed in his file or jacket explaining how he cooperated and helped the victim. It was made very clear that when he came up for parole in two years, the letter would not be a ticket out of prison but it would be a positive point in his favor. Wayne understood that the mediation could help him and couldn't hurt him, but he stated he was agreeing to do it because it was the least he could do to help Mr. Geiger. Tom explained that it was Wayne's chance to restore a sense of justice to this whole tragedy. Wayne nodded. In his own way, he understood.

After receiving permission from Wayne to share some of his thoughts with his counselor, Tom Christian returned to Mark Ackerhalt's office and told Mark that he thought that in his professional opinion, it would be a beneficial experience to conduct the mediation and that he would now talk to Gary Geiger and begin the preparation of Gary for the meeting. It was explained to Mark that the process was confidential and the meeting would only include Gary Geiger, Wayne Blanchard and Tom Christian. The only thing for public consumption would be the letter describing Wayne's cooperation and that he was helpful to the victim. (If, indeed, he was.)

Gary Geiger was anxiously awaiting the outcome of the meeting between Wayne Blanchard and Tom Christian. He had been told not to be too disappointed if Wayne wanted nothing to do with a meeting and he just wanted to do his time and get out of prison without any more hassles. When Gary received the phone call from Tom and was told it looked like a "go" he was ecstatic. He would finally be able to get his questions answered and have some peace in his life.

Soon after the visit to prison, Tom Christian received a

call from Gaby Monet from HBO. She explained how the Gary Smith and Gary Brown mediation had been so successful that HBO was doing another similar presentation and she wondered if there were any other mediations on the horizon that they could film. Apparently, HBO had two separate rape and murder cases lined up with the persons who had committed the rape and murder and a member of the victims' families. The filming would again take place in a prison setting, one in Ohio and the other in Texas. They were looking for a third case to round out their program. Tom Christian told Ms. Monet that they were working on a case of a hold up and a shooting that took place over eleven years ago. She didn't appear to be too interested, after all rape and murder cases were more sensational than a mere shooting with a surviving victim.

Tom Christian began to prepare Gary Geiger for his meeting with Wayne Blanchard. His staff observed Gary and gave their opinion on his readiness for a visit to a prison and seeing the person who had shot him. Yvonne Taylor and Mark Collins, Tom's assistant, were both good judges of character and they gave their approval after meeting Gary and talking to him in informal sessions. Tom Christian role-played with Gary giving him many different possible scenarios to respond to over a series of meetings. Finally, it was determined that Gary was ready. A phone call then came from Gaby Monet from HBO. They could not find a third case for their program so they were ready to take the robbery and shooting story but they made no promises that it would be included if it did not measure up to the other two cases.

Now permission to bring cameras into the prison would have to be obtained from the New York Department of Corrections and Gary Geiger and Wayne Blanchard would have to approve the filming of their personal, private mediation. The film could be used for training purposes and for public speaking, so the Chief Administrator of the New York Court System, Matthew Crosson, and the Community Dispute Resolution Centers Program were on board. Gary Geiger thought it over and decided his experience may help other crime victims so he signed on. Wayne Blanchard knew that it would expose him and his family to the general public, but then again, he thought it might help other young people from making some of the same mistakes he had made, so he too, approved of the filming.

The correctional officers and counselors, particularly Mark Ackerhalt, could now see the proceedings also. Tom Christian knew from experience that if people saw the power of the mediation process, the experience could open up new opportunities for other victims in need of closure and allow other offenders to see the long lasting damage their behavior had caused. It could be a great opportunity for people all over the world to see a victim and offender mediation. HBO had a vast audience. Now if the mediation would only go as it should. Every one was well prepared and whatever was going to happen would happen.

On the morning of July 20, 1992, Tom Christian and Gary Geiger were driving down the New York State Thruway to the city of Kingston (the old capitol of New York) then turning west, they took Highway 209 and proceeded into Ellenville and pulled up in front of Eastern Correctional Facility. Gary had a bottle of water and he, periodically, nervously drank from it. He couldn't sit still. Tom talked to him about the prison environment and the fact that many inmates put on a prison face when dealing with the public or anyone they were not familiar with in their day-to-day existence. Emotion is something prisoners do not often show. In order to survive, they think they have to bury their emotions and not let anyone know how they really feel. Many prefer not to have visitors because it is too hard to see the person leave and have to adjust again to the daily routine. Tom told Gary to be prepared for the cold atmosphere of cellblocks, locks, clanging gates and sterile walls and an all around confining experience. Correctional staff often will run the gamete from being very helpful and friendly to an attitude of "why are you upsetting our normal routine?". It is hard enough trying to keep a lid on hundreds of angry people without a group of do-gooders coming in to disrupt our lives. And now a camera crew is going to have to be put up with too." Tom tried to give Gary a realistic picture without frightening him. He wanted Gary to concentrate on talking to Wayne Blanchard and not be overwhelmed by the cold, sterile prison scene. Tom had Gary write down the questions that he wanted to ask Wayne. He role-played the questions and possible answers so Gary could be ready for whatever response might come from Wayne. Tom also told Gary to look at his questions when the mediation was almost over, to be sure he didn't miss anything. This probably would be his one and only opportunity to get real answers from Wayne.

As the New York State car drove through the rural countryside and finally pulled up to the prison, all the preparation had not readied Gary for the shock of the great gray walls and the imposing monstrosity of Eastern Correctional Facility. They sat in the parking lot for a while and let the experience sink in. Tom told Gary that he would be with him at all times and would not leave his side. Gary took a few deep breaths and said, "Let's do it."

They shook hands and proceeded to the main gate. Going through the visitor's center, showing identification and being walked through a metal detector were all things Gary had been told about by Tom. The correctional staff was friendly and professional. After all, Eastern Correctional Facility had a good reputation and was well run. One thing Tom did not prepare Gary for was meeting Wayne Blanchard in the hallway as he and Gary were walking to the conference room. Wayne was by himself and coming down the corridor with his head down but he was peering up through his eyebrows at the correctional officers, Tom Christian and Gary Geiger. This was not supposed to happen. Apparently, Wayne had been summoned from the prison yard because he had visitors, namely, Gary Geiger and Tom Christian. Tom Christian saw Wayne and calmly tried to keep the group walking by him and down the hallway. There was a lot of traffic coming and going so Gary Geiger was enveloped by the whole scene and did not see Wayne Blanchard go right by him.

The HBO film crew could not set up adequately in a small conference room so the auditorium and stage were selected. The mediation table would be on the stage with a chair on one side for Gary Geiger and a similar chair on the other side of the table for Wayne Blanchard. Tom Christian would sit at the end of the small table between the two. The cameras were placed on each side of the table so that the operators could look into each of the participants' eyes. The correctional officers would be on stage at the entrance to the door that Wayne Blanchard would enter. He was being detained in a room behind the stage. Mark Ackerhalt, Wayne's counselor, would be sitting in the audience with other correctional personnel. In a normal mediation in a correctional facility, the correctional officer would be stationed outside the conference room door. He or she would not hear what was being said in the confidential mediation. Because this was being filmed by HBO, all the confidentiality assurances did not apply.

It was a very hot July day and there was no air conditioning in the prison auditorium. Gary Geiger had a small towel and he was wiping his hands repeatedly as he nervously waited for HBO to get set up so the mediation could begin. It was a price all were willing to pay for this mediation to take place. Tom Christian was finally told all was set to begin the mediation. He had Gary sit on his side of the table and asked him if he was ready. As he had said before: "I am ready. I have been waiting for ten years for this. I feel prepared. Let's go for it." They shook hands again and Gary sat down. He had his small towel on his lap and his notes and a small pencil before him. He folded his hands and waited for Wayne Blanchard. Tom told Gary he would now go to the door at the back of the stage and walk Wayne Blanchard to the table. Gary nodded. His long wait was over.

Tom Christian went to the door at the back of the stage and knocked on it. Wayne Blanchard was nervously standing there between two correctional officers. He stepped into the room and Tom greeted him and asked him how he was doing. Wayne said he was doing okay. Tom asked Wayne if he was ready. He said he was. Tom had previously told Wayne he would walk him into the room and ask him to sit at his right hand at the table. Tom had told Wayne to pretend the cameras were not there and look at Mr. Geiger and himself. He shook Wayne's hand with the street style of greeting, as he had done before, to make Wayne feel Tom was there to help both him and Gary Geiger in the communication. Tom then said, "Let's do it." Tom walked Wayne to the table.

(The following dialogue is taken word for word as the participants said it. It has not been edited in any way. It was transcribed by the author from the actual HBO videotape. Reprinted with permission.)

Tom Christian: I want to thank you both for agreeing to come together today and I want to congratulate you as two human beings, two men, who can talk about a problem, an event that happened eleven years ago. It is an event that changed both of your lives. Now I am going to ask you to do two things. One, I want you to say what you really think and how you really feel. Secondly, at any time you have something to say when Gary is talking, Wayne, I want you to jot a note down if you have it. Gary, the same thing. Don't interrupt each other. Let each other talk. Now what I would like to do is have Gary tell us why he would like, after eleven years, to sit down and to talk with you, Wayne. Gary.

Gary Geiger: Eleven years I have had the need to sit and to talk with you about the incident of August '81 and I hope it can help me with the healing process. I feel because of this incident, you and I are connected right now in a negative way and perhaps today we can turn it around and make it positive. There have been many changes in my life and in your life over the last eleven years and, I think, you have been a part of my life for eleven years and possibly I have been a part of yours. I have a lot of anger and lot of frustration inside of me and it has not all been directed at you. And I have taken this frustration and anger out on some people, family and friends, that didn't quite understand what had happened to me or where I was coming from. Therefore, today I have some questions to ask of you which I just ask that you answer me straight up because anything that you say is definitely going to help me and I am sure interested in what you have to say.

Wayne Blanchard: Okay.

Tom Christian: (As planned, Tom wants to maintain a balance in the dialogue.) Wayne, you agreed to sit down and talk with Gary. Why did you do that?

Wayne Blanchard: Well, when I first heard that Mr. Geiger want (sic) this confrontation with me, I thought for a minute that I was kind of skeptical about it. Why after eleven years? Right? Then to my understanding, I was told that maybe it would help him to have this confrontation so that is why I agreed to do it.

Tom Christian: Now your counselor and I have sat down and talked with you and worked with you. I have also sat down with Gary and worked with him to prepare you for this. Now in the last eleven years, what do you think you have done to be able to help prepare yourself to come back out into the community and be a good citizen? (This question was offered to Wayne to give him a chance to tell about himself in a positive light.)

Wayne Blanchard: Well, since I have been incarcerated I have thought about a lot of things, you know. And one main reason was that when I get out of jail, I want to stay out. And so, while I been in here, I been sort of keeping myself busy with the programs that the institutions I've been in provide for one, right. The main program that I got involved with is the asbestos program. I figure when I get out I will get into that and see how far I can go with that. That is the main thing I want to do when I do get out.

Tom Christian: How about your education? You had dropped out of school, right?

Wayne Blanchard: I acquired my GED (General Education Degree or high school equivalency). I've had that for a while now. I've had pre-college (courses) and a little bit of college. And I've done a number of things... electrical, electrical work, plumbing, food service. You know, as much as I could get into, the programs that they provide for you.

Tom Christian: So you have your high school equivalency and you have made good use of the programs here in the correctional setting.

Wayne Blanchard: Yes.

Tom Christian: Okay, very good. Gary, you have questions that you feel have not been answered for eleven years that you have carried with you. I want you two to talk to each other now. This is your process. I am here just to help you and to work with you. You two now look at each other and talk to each other like two human beings, man to man.

Gary Geiger: Wayne, I mentioned in my introduction that I had some questions for you, some of which have been haunting me for eleven years and only you can provide me with the answers, if you can. Some of the other questions I have for later on have to do with yourself, but for right now, I know it is painful for you and I know it is going to be painful for me, but we have to get through this, I have to get through it to help me. I would like for you to go back with me in time to August, 1981, if you would. I know you want to forget and I want to forget, but there are just some things I have to have answered for myself so I can go on and perhaps you can go on with your life and we can close the book on this hopefully. If you would go back with me to that morning, can you tell me in your own words before you entered the motel where I worked where I was the night auditor, what were you doing that night? Do you remember? What was your state of mind? What were you going through?

Wayne Blanchard: Well, as I can recall, I was up in Arbor Hill (a low income neighborhood in Albany, New York) and a few people came by in a car to tell me that they knew where some money was at. Right? So I asked a couple of questions of them and then I got into the car and we came down to the Best Western there where you were at. My state of mind, I really can't remember. Right? But that is what transpired. So they picked me up and told me where the money was at. At the time I hadn't been working. I was just out there, in the streets just roaming, and we came down to the Best Western and, like I said, everything happened.

Gary Geiger: Thank you for answering that. Now had you ever been to the motel before?

Wayne Blanchard: No.

Gary Geiger: Never? Did we know each other before? Did we ever see each other before?

Wayne Blanchard: Not that I know of, no.

Gary Geiger: Now this part is very tricky for me as well as for you. This is part of the questions that I have said have been haunting me. When we were inside the motel and two men approached me at the desk and two men fanned out, one to my left and one to my right, I knew right away what was coming down immediately. I knew what was going to happen. But what I want to ask you, if you can possibly help me with this, is why did the robbery get so violent? Why did it escalate so much when I complied in every way to what you wanted? I gave you the money. Why the gun butts to my head and the fists to my face and ripping my glasses off and tearing the inside of my eye? (Gary took off his glasses at this point and rubbed the corner of his eye.) Why did it escalate so much?

Wayne Blanchard: Okay. From what I can recall, I never hit you with my gun butt. Right? My intentions were to come there and get the money and leave. Right? But, I guess, you know maybe some of the people that were with me were violent, violent people. You know, I guess, there were a couple of times where somebody had said for you to do something like get on the floor or something to that effect, and I guess you hesitated. Maybe they were a little afraid of you because you were a kind of muscular then, kind of big and stocky. Well, as far as anybody else, I can't say why they did it, but if you are really looking for the reason I shot you, I can tell you that.

Tom Christian: Were the people under the influence of alcohol or any other drugs at the time or was everybody straight?

Wayne Blanchard: No, I had been drinking and smoking (dope) that night. When I got into the car, maybe there was some beer bottles. Maybe there was, yeah, possibly, yeah.

Gary Geiger: You said something a few minutes ago that I just want to clarify when I said the gun butts to the head. You are saying that somebody else also in the party had a gun?

Wayne Blanchard: Yes.

Gary Geiger: (Visibly shaken) Did I represent something that you hated? I mean, did I do something? Were you angry that night, angry at somebody? Did I just happen to be there?

Wayne Blanchard: You didn't do, I see, nothing to anger me. In fact, I didn't know you until that night. I didn't see you until that night. No, you didn't do anything to anger me.

Gary Geiger: When, if you remember, I was on the floor, you brought me into the backroom where there was carpeting and I was on the floor. I don't know if yourself saw it but maybe other people saw it. The door wasn't locked and there was a locked safe in there. I think what happened was you got excited. You thought there was more money to be had. And, if you remember, you came to me and you put the gun to my head and you asked for the combination to the safe. One of the questions that has been bothering me is first did you believe me when I told you I didn't have the combination?

Wayne Blanchard: Okay, let me clarify it for you. I never put my gun to your head. See, that wasn't me. All the time I was in the background when this was happening. I was sort of a lookout while everybody was doing what they had to do. And I just mentioned that there was another gun there, an individual with a gun, but that wasn't me who put the gun to your head.

Tom Christian: Did you see someone put the gun to his head?

Wayne Blanchard: Oh, yes.

Tom Christian: Okay.

Gary Geiger: They put the gun to my head a second time also and this time it was cocked and I was asked again for the combination to the safe and in my most sincerest voice I said, 'I don't have it.' I thought at that time that they were going to shoot me in the head.

Wayne Blanchard: If you can recall, when you said you did not know the combination to the safe and you were only the night auditor, somebody said, 'Okay, let's get out of here.'

Gary Geiger: They said, 'Knock him out'.

Wayne Blanchard: Yeah, right, that too. 'Let's get out of here.' That's when we had left.

Gary Geiger: Somebody hit me in the back of the head at that time and you say it was not you that hit me in the back of the head.

Wayne Blanchard: No.

Gary Geiger: I went to the floor I was pretending that I was knocked out and you are saying that at that time when I was hit in the back of the head by some one else, you were gone. You had already left. You were gone?

Wayne Blanchard: No, I didn't leave. I was like a background lookout. I was there where the door leads to the little office. I was in that area.

Gary Geiger: You did see somebody actually hit me in the back of the head then to knock me out?

Wayne Blanchard: Yes, I did.

Gary Geiger: The next thing I remember is I heard steps running away and if you remember the carpeting (There was shag carpeting in the office and linoleum in the hallway) and I was nervous. I was hit by the gun butt, and I was bleeding from the head, and I instinctively jumped up. At that time I heard a loud explosion and I bent over and I felt a burning sensation in my stomach. You fired that shot?

Wayne Blanchard: Yes, I did.

Gary Geiger: Can you tell me, please, why you shot me?

Wayne Blanchard: Okay, somebody said, 'Let's get out of here.' The running noise you heard must have been us leaving. Something told me in my head to go back and check you. So when I came back into the room, I found that you were getting up and going to a box on the wall. I thought that it was an alarm that you were running to. It would have hindered our escape so I called to you and I said, 'Hey!' And when you turned around, that's when I fired the shot and then I ran.

Gary Geiger: Did you try to kill me?

Wayne Blanchard: No. I believe that if I had any intentions of actually killing you, I would have fired more than one shot. That shot was more to get your attention from where I thought you were heading.

Gary Geiger: Did you think of firing a second shot when I ran towards the door? If you remember there was a blue door in front of me that was locked. I tried to run through the door and I bounced off. Did you think about firing another time?

Wayne Blanchard: (hesitating) I can't remember that part. I fired one shot and I ran.

Gary Geiger: Those questions have been bothering me. I

didn't know about the second gun. I thought you were the only one that had a gun that night. And I didn't know that someone else put the gun to my head. The other thing I want to clarify is that the motel was old. There was no alarm system. If there was an alarm system, I would have hit it right then and there. I knew what was going down. When I jumped up I was just scared. I was not heading for an alarm system or anything like that. Yes, after you left I did make a phone call. I called the bus station next door to tell them I had just been robbed and shot. I couldn't even remember the telephone number of the police department. (As stated before, 911 was not available at that time.) That's how confused I was. I was hurt. My glasses were tore off. I had to feel my way from the back room to the front of the motel. I had a burning sensation in my right quadrant in my stomach and I was feeling my way to the front. But there was absolutely no alarm. Again, those questions have been bothering me since that night. Again, you are looking at me and looking me straight in the eye and you told me that you're not the one who put the gun to my head and you did admit that you shot me. I accept that. It was quite scary. I had other problems down there. I had problems down there in the bar. I was my own security. Sometimes I took it upon myself to help the barmaid out if she had a problem with a drunken patron. But I never expected any thing like this. And to go back again, I know it's painful but I did comply in every way but I do admit that I did hesitate when I was told to get down. All I thought was take what you want and leave. It wasn't my money. I would have helped you to the car with it. They were insured. I was just worried about myself. I just wanted you to take what you wanted and go. I had nothing against you. I didn't even know you. You admitted that I didn't do anything. I had been a banker years ago and the training helped me. I guess it did. I am here.

Before I ask you any more questions, I want you to know what a victim of a violent crime goes through after the incident. It just doesn't end with the incident. The pain goes on. And I said in the beginning that I have anger and it is not all directed at you. I had anger in the courtroom. You were on trial. I was on the stand for two and one half hours and it was ninety degrees. I was treated like I was a piece of meat. I felt like I was handcuffed in there. The questions from your attorney about my lifestyle being scrutinized. Was I sleeping on the job? How could I identify anyone if I had my glasses off? One of her statements I will never forget. 'Aren't you relishing in all this publicity, Mr. Geiger? Isn't this what you wanted your whole life?'

Yeah, I wanted a bullet in me. It wasn't fun for me up there. I was under strict orders not to say a word to you. I was only ordered to talk about what I saw, not my feelings.

Wayne Blanchard: Did the district attorney tell you anything about that he wanted me to go through with this trial? Because I was actually trying to get a cop-out. But he wouldn't let me cop-out.

Tom Christian: You were looking for a reduced plea? You were ready to admit to the crime?

Wayne Blanchard: Yes, I was ready to take a plea but they just wouldn't let me. (The district attorney's office must have felt that they had a strong case and an eyewitness and they could go for a longer sentence.)

Gary Geiger: I was told very little. I was told to just say what I saw. I wanted to say more. I had feelings. I wanted to talk to you for a few minutes. I was told that if I said anything like that they would have to start all over again. I felt shackled. With the line of questioning, I felt I had done something wrong. I felt guilty. I walked off that stand and I was angry. And frankly, at the time, I wanted to go after you because I was so angry. But I stood there and I looked and I said, 'This is not the way to do it. Two wrongs do not make a right. I just have to let the system take care of it.' The point I am trying to make is that the pain doesn't stop at the incident. Too many times victims don't come forward. They are afraid of the system. They don't testify. I felt I had an obligation. I was there. I was a witness. We victims have names. We have jobs. We have families. We have lives. I had every right to be there that night. I was an innocent person.

Tom Christian: Wayne, Gary has shared some of his feelings at the trial. When you were sitting there and you wanted to plead guilty and they wouldn't accept your plea what were you thinking and feeling?

Wayne Blanchard: At first, I wanted to get it all over with, the trial, everything. Sitting in the county jail, you get to thinking. I actually did not want to go to trial. It appeared to me that they made me go to trial. They wanted me to go to trial. While I was sitting at the defense table, it all seemed like a circus to me. They displayed me to the jury. Do you recall when the D.A. stood you (Gary) in front of me and you started shaking. I realized that you were actually afraid but then I thought it was courtroom dramatics. To sum it all up, it all seemed like a circus to me because I wanted to cop-out and admit to the crime. I didn't want to go through that part of it at all. I can understand how Mr. Geiger felt then and feels now.

Tom Christian: Are you (Gary Geiger) interested in what happened after the crime when they got back in the car and took off? What happened after that? (Gary nods, yes.)

Wayne Blanchard: One of the individuals who was in the car, we went to his address. I stayed at his house for about an hour to an hour and one half. I did not get back into his car. When he got back, I asked where everybody went and he told me and then I left and went home. Even that same night, the police stopped me and questioned me about where I had been and where I was coming from and so forth and so on. Me, myself, I left town. I was on parole at the time. I left town because I was scared and I was hoping that you didn't pass away. I realized I had shot you and that was a possibility. All the time, I was listening to the news and they said you were in stable condition. I was very happy that you did not pass away. They didn't see me again until I was apprehended me (sic) in Illinois. It was not for another crime. It was just that I didn't have identification. That's when they brought me back and started the trial and everything. They had another individual (in jail) who was convicted of the same crime and he was going through his trial (Goldie Jackson) and they were starting his trial. After that they came (to jail) and arrested me and took me to trial.

Gary Geiger: Thank you for telling me what happened after the crime. One more thing: during the trial. When I was in front of you, it wasn't a ploy. It was me. I wanted to stand in front of you. I wasn't afraid. As far as the shaking, I was angry. I wanted to show you that, 'hey, I am here. I didn't die. I am here and I am man enough to stand in front of you.' It wasn't a ploy, it was just my way of letting you know that ' here I am'. Now, I know that you have lost a lot. You have been incarcerated for eleven years and nothing can take that back. We have already touched on what you have done in prison but let me tell you what I lost. I lost quite a bit. When I was physically recovering from my wounds, I went through stages. I hated the nightfall. I hated the night to come. I would see the incident over and over and over again. Walking in, going around me, the shot, everything. Over and over again. It got so bad that I actually went back to the motel and restaged the whole thing with the employees' help to see if there was some way that I could have escaped. We reenacted it three times in a row, and every single time, I got caught. That was my mind saying that maybe I could have done something to have gotten away. I was going through this thing with nightmares for a long time. I would get up in the middle of the night and start shaking, uncontrollable shaking from head to toe. I couldn't stop. I wondered, 'Am I always going to be like this? Is this ever going to end? What's going on? What is the matter with me?' I never had this before in my life. I didn't know what was happening to me. It was more the mental part than it was the physical. Every time I worked out, every time I moved, I thought the bullet was going to move, which is still in my body. I went to three or four different surgeons who assured me that, well, you get four different opinions: 'No, it won't move;' 'yes, it might move;' 'maybe it might move', 'maybe it won't move.' But in my mind I didn't know; therefore, I kept wondering if I was going to be the same person as I was before. Maybe you don't know this, but at the time I was a nationally ranked athlete. I was a nationally ranked weight lifter and then I went back to running, a sprinter. I just finished fourth in the national championships and I took the night job at the motel so I could train during the day because I wanted that year to be my year to win or place at the nationals so I could, number one, get a sponsor, and number two, I could get a coaching job. That's why I took the job at night so I could do the books at night and I could also do my training during the day. Well, with everything going on it took me three years to get back into my sport, and by that time, I had lost too much speed. I couldn't get it back. It has taken me until now to get my national ranking back. People look at me now and they say,' Gee, at your age you are pretty fast.'

I say 'thank you' to them, but eleven years ago I was really fast. This is just a shell of what I was. I was in my own prison. I had lost a lot too. Then, to compound that, when I was recovering from my physical injuries, I called the motel and told them I was ready to come back, not at night but during the day. They said, 'Mr. Geiger, we are sorry but we talked to the home office and due to the publicity, you no longer have a job. But we will approve your unemployment benefits.'

Thanks a lot. Now I no longer have a job, I am going through nightmares and a loss of identity and now I am going through guilt feelings. I kept thinking the whole thing was my fault. How could I be so selfish to have taken a job like this? How could I have put myself in jeopardy? Maybe it was my fault that this happened. Maybe I did something in my past that I did to deserve this. Maybe this is the way life evens out. Now something happened to me. I was even now. I said, 'No.'

But that's the way victims think. They feel guilty all the time. It wasn't my fault. I was innocent. I was defenseless. It was not my fault. Now, I literally took the phone book and went down a list of doctors to help me get over this loss of identity and anxiety attacks. Not one doctor would help me. Not one, because number one, I was a compensation case, and, number two, I didn't have a job. I had to sell my car. I had to take a room at the YMCA. I had to start from scratch. I know that being incarcerated and being out of the life stream for eleven years has not been a lot of fun for you either. But I was also in my own prison too. This was one of the reasons I had to come and see you.

Tom Christian: Wayne, do you have any feelings or reactions to that?

Wayne Blanchard:(looking very sincere) Yes, I would like to say something to Mr. Geiger. Eleven years is sort of a hell, right? But I am truly sorry for what happened in that motel that night. I am not only sorry for the pain that you feel but for what your family had to go through and what had led up to what your life it is now. If I had it to do all over again, it would never have happened. As far as the bullet being inside of you, there is nothing I can do about it now except say I am sorry and I really am. And that is the main reason that I told Mr. Christian that I accepted to have this confrontation with you. If there was something I could do or say that could help you put it behind you, I would be glad to do it. That is why I am here today, and again, I am truly sorry for what happened that night.

Gary Geiger: (appearing relieved) Wayne, I have been waiting eleven years to hear that. It takes a real man to admit when they are wrong and apologize as you just did. I didn't know if I was ever going to hear that. I tried six years ago to have this but I didn't get very far. I am glad that you are sorry. I had forgiven you a long time ago for what had happened. I didn't forget because I have the bullet in my body, possibly, until I die. But part of my anger was not directed at you but at the parole system. You were on parole at the time for another offense, and they just took you and literally threw you out on the street. You didn't have any job. You didn't have any money, and as you admitted here today, all you were doing was just wandering around and I happened to get in the way. But, you see, when innocent people get in the way, there is always an aftermath. I think, possibly, you understand that now. I think this may have led to that crime. You were just not ready to go into the job stream. How are you different today? Can you tell me how you are different today than you were at twenty-one? Do you have any more anger in you?

Wayne Blanchard: As far as you were concerned, I never had any animosity towards you at all. I know I did you a wrong and you had to do what you had to do. You had to come to court. You had to testify. All the time I have been in jail, I have never been angry at you. You have done nothing to me. And as far as you maybe believing that I had some animosity towards you for doing all this time and getting out and coming looking for you and this and that. No! That is the furthest thing from my mind. Like you, I want to put all this behind me. I want to go ahead with my life. I have been in jail for quite some time now. This is not my first bit. On the first one I did just about five years. I had been out four months before this incident took place. I was twenty-one years old at the time and I really didn't have much on my mind. I was just out there, no responsibility or nothing. Now I am thirty-two years old and I have had time to think and figure out what I am going to do with the rest of my life. Crime is not a part of it. I am finished with that. I realized I did a lot of stupid things and this being the main silly thing I did in my life. I was sort of young back then with nothing on my mind. I was just out there roaming and at the rate I was going had I not been sent away, maybe I would have ended up dead. So I can say that this time has actually helped me. It really has.

Gary Geiger: When I talk to people about this meeting, if there are twenty people, ten would think I am crazy, the other ten are supportive. What you are saying is that inmates can be rehabilitated.

Wayne Blanchard: Today, I would like to say this. What I call my first bit, you can come in here and see it as a joke, just get involved in all the negative things. But this time, when I come in here, of the programs that were offered to me, these people in the institution, the State, they can't make you do nothing. It is up to you. It is up to the individual. The programs are there. It is up to you to take advantage of them. That's what I did, as opposed to the first time. I came up with no responsibility but that's just not me any more. I don't live that way anymore.

Tom Christian: There are a lot of young people out in the communities, they are shooting each other. Violence has probably escalated in the past eleven years since you were out there. Can you make some kind of commitment to Gary that when you get out there you are going to be helping people, not hurting people? If you could talk to a young person now, what would you tell him?

Wayne Blanchard: I am from Arbor Hill, that is a section in Albany that is terrible around there. When I get out I would like to say a lot to the youth that's roaming the streets the same way I was. From my experience, I will let them know that this is no fun doing time out of your life for doing something that is really silly.

Tom Christian: Will you be thinking of Gary Geiger when you talk to them?

Wayne Blanchard: I am trying to put this behind me.

Tom Christian: It is behind you, but when a kid says you don't know what you re talking about, will you think of Gary Geiger and try harder?

Wayne Blanchard: Sure, I will be telling them to stay in school and all.

Tom Christian: You know what it is going to be like when you get back in your environment, your community? All your friends and old partners will pat you on the back, feel sorry for you and all that, and you are going to go back there and then have somebody say to you, ' Let's go get some money, or 'do you want to try a little crack or smoke dope.

What can you say to Gary that will prevent you from jumping back and in four months you will not be back in the same life style?

Wayne Blanchard: What can I say? (looking straight at Gary and hesitating) The only thing I can say is that with me, this will never happen again. I have learned more than a lesson. Things that I was doing in my teens and twenties, I am just more focused now. There was nothing for me before, I was just out there. I am really tired of this. I don't want to put up with this anymore. I would like to make a definite change in my life for the positive. I have been going through this for too long. I have a lot of pain in me as well from all this. My life has been jail, jail, jail. I really haven't had a chance to live my life out in society because of the stupid things I did.

Gary Geiger: You have a real chance to turn it around when you get out. You can be a role model for these kids because I drive down in that area on business sometimes and I see these kids on school days hanging out on the stoops at ten o'clock in the morning. I am saying to myself, 'what are you doing, you are never going to get out of this if you don't stay in school'. They are looking up to those people on the corner selling crack and what ever. You could come out of here and you can turn every thing that has happened to you negatively in life and make it something positive. There are centers in the area that you grew up in and you could go there and talk to the kids. How would you feel if a young person came up to you in few years time and said, 'Gee, Wayne, remember when I met you? I was headed for trouble. You talked to us and told us what you went through and it helped straighten me out and steered me in the right direction. I stayed in school, I got a job and I just want to thank you.'

How would that make you feel? You have the opportunity to do it because I am told that you are looked up to by the other inmates in here. That tells me that you have a gift, a way with people. You can use it. Get out of here and you are going to get out soon, I imagine. And you can really change your life right around and you can help kids. What if you helped two or three kids see the positive way instead of the way you took. That is going to make a world of difference. You are going to feel good about yourself. If you feel good about yourself, you will never come in here again. Our lives, like I said in the beginning, paralleled each other. I had a violent upbringing, too. I wasn't born rich, I came from a relatively poor family, dysfunctional family. I was headed down the wrong path too, but I choose the other path. I am not saying I didn't do some bad things, but I choose the positive path. And I think my sports and liking myself really helped and kept me from being in trouble. I know who I am. As soon as you know who Wayne Blanchard is and you get some self-esteem and you help people, you are going to feel good. I help people now. I try to give back. I do some personal training. I do some coaching. I try to help other victims and it made me feel good.

Wayne Blanchard: I would like to do that.

Gary Geiger: What are your goals when you get out, further your education?

Wayne Blanchard: My main goal, as I say, I enjoy doing asbestos work. I got into it and I really like it. I am a worker, a class "A" handler. I would like to go on and be a supervisor and maybe even go further in the asbestos thing. .

Gary Geiger: I have a friend in that field and you can make some money. In fact, they just found some asbestos in our area not too long ago. Hopefully, when you get out, you can hook up with that as well as working in the community. I tell you, Wayne, they need help. It is different today than it was eleven years ago. The kids are in trouble. They really are. They are ending up dead because they want the quick money. You wanted the quick money. Look what happened. You changed my life forever. Your life changed. My family's lives. But you could turn that around and work with these kids because they need a role model, somebody to look up to. They will listen to you because you have been through it. I know you can do it.

Tom Christian: Is there anything else, Wayne, you would like to say to Gary? Any other questions that you might have, concerns or feelings that you might want to share with him now?

Wayne Blanchard:(now sweating profusely) I would like to thank you, too, for coming here today and facing me after what I did to you, right. I just want to say again that I am very sorry and I hope that your life gets a lot better than what it is now.

Gary Geiger: I think today is definitely going to be a step in the right direction for me and, I hope, for you. You have had hard times and sometimes you say you feel different from other people. Well, sometimes I feel different than other people. Sometimes I feel like I don't belong. I feel like I have a sign above me. I can't see it, and it says 'victim of a violent crime, proceed with caution'. I don't know why but sometimes people are afraid of me or intimidated by me because they know what happened to me. They don't understand what happened. I feel kind of unique, I went through this and not many people do and survive. I just feel I have to be some kind of a spokesman, somebody to speak out about this. Like I said, we were connected negatively for the last eleven years. I think now we have a better understanding of each other and we are more positive. If Wayne doesn't have anything else to say, what I would like to say to him is that the last time you and I met, you had your hand extended to me in anger. Now I would like to extend my hand to you as a sign of healing. (Gary Geiger stands up and extends his hand to Wayne Blanchard. Wayne rises and takes Gary's hand and again thanks him for coming.)

Tom Christian: (also joins them standing) Thank you both, very good job. (The mediation is over, and Tom walks Wayne back to the correctional officer at the door. The correctional officer unlocks the door and they go out into the hallway. Tom shakes Wayne's hand with the two-fold grip.) Great job, man. It took a lot of guts. You did it. Gary wants to talk to you informally for a few minutes.

Gary Geiger: (Wayne comes back into the room and is brought over to Gary.) Wayne, were you straight with me with all your answers?

Wayne Blanchard: Yes, yes, indeed. Like I said, I realized what I had done to you was terribly wrong.

Gary Geiger: I didn't know there were two guns.

Wayne Blanchard: Yes, there were two guns.

Gary Geiger: My sister and family said I shouldn't do this. They couldn't even talk about this. They said you were just going to lie. But I looked right into your eyes and you were not lying. I am a pretty good judge of character and you were telling the truth. And I really meant it when I said you could help these kids. They are in trouble. They really are. You don't want to see them in here.

Wayne Blanchard: In my neighborhood, I know, calling home and reading the Schenectady and Albany papers, I see the trends.

Gary Geiger: Maybe we can meet again when you get out.

Wayne Blanchard: I would like that.

Gary Geiger: Thanks a lot, Wayne. I really appreciate it, man.

Wayne Blanchard: Thank you, too. (The two men embrace and Wayne says,' Alright' and Wayne begins the walk back to his cellblock with a real spring in his step. One can see he feels good about himself and the meeting.)

Tom Christian shook Gary Geiger's hand and congratulated him on an outstanding job. The crew from HBO and the correctional personnel, especially Mark Ackerhalt, Wayne Blanchard's counselor, were very pleased with the outcome. Tom Christian and Gary Geiger rode back to Albany, and on the way, debriefed the mediation. Gary was very relieved and very happy. He felt he was reaching a sense of closure and a feeling of peace, at last.

In a victim and offender mediation, a follow-up visit with the people involved usually occurs about a month after the mediation. This allows the individuals involved a chance to think about the effects of the meeting and talk about how it influenced their lives. In Gary Geiger's case, he was living in Scotia, New York, next to Albany, so follow up meetings were easy to schedule. Gary Geiger stated that he was now more at peace with himself, and his concerns and worries were answered by Wayne's straightforward approach to the encounter.

In traveling back to Eastern Correctional Facility, Tom Christian met with Wayne Blanchard and was pleased with Wayne's attitude and responses. Wayne appeared relieved and at ease with the meeting and was very comfortable with the results. Mark Ackerhalt thought the benefit to Gary Geiger was very evident. He was more skeptical about the long lasting effect on Wayne Blanchard. He figured time would tell if Wayne just went back to the prison population with life as usual or if it would truly influence his behavior. Being institutionalized for so long it would take more than an hour-long mediation to change his behavior.

The question still had to be answered as to how the filming by HBO would affect all involved. The Gary Geiger and Wayne Blanchard mediation was being placed in with two other mediations from other states, Ohio and Texas. They were gruesome rape and murder cases, and although HBO had initially thought that the Gary Geiger and Wayne

Blanchard mediation might be too mild for their consideration, after the taping, the producer, Gaby Monet, thought it might be the best story of the three. It definitely was the more complete and true mediation.

The Gary Geiger Story became the centerpiece for the HBO presentation called, Confronting Evil. The television program went on to be selected as a finalist for an Ace Award for outstanding docudrama. It would lose out to Educating Henry, a story of a person with mental retardation; however, the program was shown on HBO a number of times, and people from all over the world would write and comment on the show.

Wayne Blanchard received fan mail from a number of women, and one person came all the way from Amsterdam, Holland, to visit Wayne in prison and began a short relationship with him. Wayne's good looks and sincerity evidently turned her head. Wayne, however, also suffered some repercussions for participating in the filming. He was called Mr. HBO by some of the correctional officers and inmates. He was also cornered by some of his peers in the institution who wanted a piece of the money he received from HBO for allowing the taping. He was not paid anything for his role but the confronting element was not easily convinced.

Tom Christian and Gary Geiger had Gary's video taped mediation separated from the other two mediations (rapes and murders) and it was labeled The Gary Geiger Story. This portion of the program is being used for numerous speaking engagements in schools and community program. (See Chapter 8)

The New York Court System, through the Community Dispute Resolution Centers Program, uses The Gary Geiger Story video for their training needs; in fact, it was at the request of many of the trainees that the full story of Gary Geiger and Wayne Blanchard came to be written in this book format.

CHAPTER SEVEN

PAROLE

Parole is a condition that can be used in the correctional system to help alleviate overcrowded prisons or to give the offender an opportunity to prove that he or she can function in society after having served a portion of one's original sentence in a correctional facility. The person released from prison before the full sentence has been served will be supervised by an individual called a parole agent or parole officer. This supervision can be in a residential halfway house (halfway between prison and the community) or in the community within the person's own living arrangements. Supervision can be intense, as often as daily reporting, or it can require the parolee to be seen weekly or monthly. The parolee can be in a community drug or counseling program and the parole agent will work with the program staff to assist the parolee. Employment is very important to help the parolee earn money and begin to be fully integrated back into the community. The parole agent can counsel the parolee on job interviewing and maintaining a job. Transportation is very important for the parolee to make it to work on time, every day and begin building good work habits. Sometimes a thing as simple as an alarm clock and a bus schedule can make all the difference in the world.

The person on parole can also just be on paper and have little or no reporting restrictions. The individual may also be fitted with an electronic ankle or wrist bracelet that will monitor movements. The parole agent can call the person's home and the parolee must answer the phone, showing that they are there, or be considered in violation of parole. Parole is open to the potential and creative methods of a given agency or parole officer.

The incarcerated prisoner normally has to appear before a parole board to be considered for release to parole. The parole board members are usually political appointments by the governor of the state. A parole board member may or may not have experience in the field of corrections. In recent years, parole boards have been rather conservative in releasing prisoners because they do not want to be responsible for letting a person out who may then commit a new, serious violent crime. Michael Dukakis found that out the hard way when George Bush Senior made it known that Willie Horton had been released to a program on Dukakis's watch and then committed rape and murder. Some say that event may have been the start of Dukakis's loss of the election.

It was in this atmosphere that Wayne Blanchard became eligible for parole because he had served the minimum of his twelve and one half to twenty-five year sentence. Gary Geiger had been so impressed with Wayne Blanchard's attitude during the mediation that he asked if he could appear before the New York State Parole Board to speak in favor of Wayne's release on parole. The New York Parole Board does not allow a person to appear before them but they do permit a person to write to a member of the board and then talk to that one member. That person can then bring the request to the full board. With all the information from Wayne Blanchard's prison file and his counselor's report, the board then studied the material and made a decision. Normally, in a case involving violence, the board rejects the request the first time a person comes up before them. In Wayne Blanchard's case, the parole board had a letter stating that Wayne had cooperated in helping the victim of his crime through the mediation from the Community Dispute Resolution Centers Program of the New York State Unified Court System. He also had a letter from the victim of his crime, Gary Geiger, stating that he was in favor of releasing Wayne Blanchard on parole. The parole board then reviewed all the information and voted to release Wayne Blanchard on parole.

There are conditions with parole, and they vary depending on the person and the parole agent. The parolee is still accountable on paper for the full sentence and if conditions are not met or a new crime is committed, that person can be returned to prison for a portion or all of his or her original sentence. (This is called a revocation.)

Tom Christian played on a New York State softball team. One of his team members was John Collins who ran an asbestos removal company. Wayne Blanchard was trained in asbestos removal. John Collins said he was always looking for good employees so he was willing to hire Wayne Blanchard. Prior to Wayne's release, Tom contacted John Collins to set up the job opportunity. It is very important that a new parolee have a job to keep him busy and give him a regular paycheck. Once a parolee is off to a good start, he has a much better chance to keep going in the right direction. It is called the inertia theory; however, it can work the other way also. If a parolee does not get going in the community, he can go backwards into old friends and old behaviors, and then inertia keeps him going the wrong way.

John Collins informed Tom that his shop had recently gone union and he would not be able to hire Wayne Blanchard as he had thought he might.

Another major tragedy was also awaiting Wayne when he was released. His brother, John Blanchard, had been arrested for a double homicide. He was soon convicted of killing an elderly, Polish immigrant couple who lived in his neighborhood. Evidently, John was addicted to crack cocaine and entered the couple's home to steal items to sell to buy crack. He was so high that he was careless and seen in the area. An arrest was immediate and conviction was swift. Now Wayne not only had a brother who was a New York State trooper but he also had a brother who was serving life in prison.

While Wayne was serving his time, he had married and being allowed conjugal visits, had fathered a child, Wayne Jr. Unfortunately, Wayne Jr. had developed cancer and Wayne Sr. had looked forward to being a parent to his child and provide support for him. His wife, Angela, had other ideas. She wanted a divorce and didn't want anything to do with Wayne Sr. She did allow visitation but wanted Wayne to come at scheduled times.

Being institutionalized for so many years, Wayne began to have immediate problems functioning in his new found society. He was still shaking the prison dust off of himself. He was used to three hots (meals) and a cot (bed). He was programmed to respond to bells and the prison routine and schedule. He made major efforts to obtain employment. He began painting with another brother but it was a contract job and when the work was completed, Wayne was again out of work. He took small jobs and even painted for Yvonne Taylor from the court system. She needed work done on her home and tried to help Wayne.

Wayne began to drink and stated that beer was like "drinking water." Tom Christian tried to encourage Wayne to not drink any alcohol for two years until he had established himself back in the community. As is common with alcoholics, he claimed he could handle booze and knew when to quit.

Gary Geiger met with Wayne on a number of occasions

and tried to encourage him to work on a regular basis. He also had friends hire Wayne to do painting jobs for them. Wayne began to wear his hat cocked sideways and his pants half-mast, just like the homeboys in his hood. He was reliving the years of his youth that he had missed being in prison.

In one discussion, Wayne admitted slapping his ex-wife Angie when they disagreed on the visitation schedule. He was counseled and told that kind of behavior was an assault and he could have his parole revoked. He was still living back in the old days when he thought he could "slap the bitch" when he felt he wasn't shown respect. Domestic violence was not tolerated as just a family matter within the community, the police, prosecutor and the court system. It was treated now, as it should be, as an assault.

The *Albany Times Union* had followed the Gary Geiger and Wayne Blanchard story with a keen human interest slant; however, its next story on Wayne Blanchard was an accusation of rape. Everyone who was interested in this case now wondered if the mediation and all the publicity around this matter had been worth it. Wayne Blanchard was now back in the Albany County Jail.

Wayne Blanchard had been on his way over to visit his son, when he ran into his wife. His story was that they had an argument over the visitation schedule and Angie seeing other men while Wayne Jr. was present in the home. Angie didn't want Wayne to come over unannounced. She accused him of rape to keep him from interfering with her social life. The police report stated that Angie was walking down the street with a male friend, and Wayne Blanchard came up and confronted them. He was jealous and told the other man to take a hike, which he did, fearing Wayne's physical demeanor and prison reputation. Wayne then backed Angie into the alley by their house and said, " You know what I want." The police report went on to allege that Wayne put Angie against the wall and tore her panties and raped her.

She went to the hospital for an examination and the hospital medical personnel verified intercourse had taken place and her undergarments were ripped. The evidence looked overwhelming.

Tom Christian visited Wayne in the detention center. He informed Wayne that he could have gone to Family Court and received a visitation schedule that he and Angie could both agree upon. Wayne stated any intercourse was consensual and denied the rape but did admit to slapping Angie once. It did not look good for Wayne.

Gary Geiger was interviewed on television about the allegations and he stood behind Wayne. He stated that Wayne was innocent until proven guilty. Gary's co-workers stopped talking to him, and people who knew him questioned how he could support a rapist. Gary's family also received negative reactions to Gary's behavior. Gary went to see Wayne with members of Wayne's family, and his belief in Wayne's innocence grew. A number of parole meetings were scheduled to possibly revoke Wayne's parole; however, Angie failed to show up to testify. After Wayne spent three months in the detention facility, Angie sent a note with her notarized signature to Gary via Wayne's brother stating that she wanted to drop the charges. She said she just wanted Wayne not to bother her again. Gary brought the note to the senior parole officer. It read:

District Attorney's Office
Albany County
Att: Veronica Dumas,

I am writing this letter in reference to the charges filed against my husband Wayne Blanchard. From the beginning I was repeatedly pressured into filing the charges. Some one other then(sic) myself called the police and got them involved. I feel as though this is and always has been a husband and wife matter. On the night of question I felt no need to go to the hospital, but five or six members of the police department pressured me relentlessly to go to the hospital, I finally coul'nt (sic) deal with the pressure anymore so I went to the hospital. While at the hospital Det. Paul Goldberg was after me telling him several times over and over again that I did not want to sign statements against my husband. But after hours of more relentless pressure I couldn't take it no more and so I gave in.

So what I am trying to say to you is that I never said at any time that I was raped. Therefore, I feel as though the charges should not be pursued any further.

Angela Blanchard (signed above the printed name).
State of New York
City of Albany

Before me came in person Angela Blanchard this 15th day of March 1995.
Benjamin G. Garland (signature above name)
Notary Public, State of New York
No.4666242
Qualified in Albany County
Commission Expires April 30,1996

Two days later the charges were dropped. A child visitation schedule was worked out with the court and Wayne was ordered not to have any contact with Angie. What really happened between Angie and Wayne would remain between them. Was it a case of domestic violence and rape or was it a police department pressuring a wife to get her parolee husband off the streets? After all, Wayne had received a lot of positive publicity helping his past crime victim Gary Geiger. This may not have set well with some law enforcement individuals. In any case, this time Wayne was targeted, but he was able to dodge the bullet. While on parole, Wayne never was able to "get it together." He was sent to programs to address his addictive behavior, but he would attend for a while and then decide that he could do it on his own, only to fail again. He would be revoked off parole by the court at the recommendation of his parole officer a number of times and returned to prison. Each time he would forget his best intentions and return to his former behaviors. The question arose whether being institutionalized for close to sixteen years put him into a rut that he couldn't climb out of. Many people who serve prison terms cannot adjust to modern day society. The young woman from Amsterdam, Holland, who came from overseas to visit Wayne before he was released began a relationship with Wayne while he was on parole. It didn't last very long. Wayne said she was too demanding and controlling. She went back to Europe. A theory regarding people who are incarcerated is that they cannot form lasting relationships easily. They don't trust people, particularly themselves. With a relationship comes responsibility and this is something they don't feel comfortable working on over a period of time.

Wayne would have a number of women in his life but none of them would last or help him turn his lifestyle around. He would live off them for a period of time and then go on to someone else. In one case, he fathered another child with a woman who held a responsible job as a nurse.

Gary Geiger and Tom Christian would become discouraged by Wayne's behavior, but they always concluded that Wayne was still a work in progress. Other than the rape accusation from his wife, which was dropped, Wayne was not accused of any new crime. The mediation process had helped him immensely, he stated, but the follow up was marred by unemployment problems and his use of mind-altering drugs. Justice was not quite restored in his life. An incident while he was on parole, however, would bring him to a crossroads. He would witness a drive by shooting and be forced to make a decision to come forward or fade off into the neighborhood and let the chaos continue.

CHAPTER EIGHT

JUSTICE RESTORED

When a person commits a criminal act, there are consequences. The act affects the lives of many people. It is just not the offender who must face the reality of what has happened but also the victim, the victim's family, neighbors and friends, the offenders family, neighbors and friends, the members of the criminal justice system (police, prosecutors, detention facilities staff and the court personnel). In short, a criminal act affects the entire community. It is not enough to simply punish the offender and ignore the rest of the community. Often this is exactly what is done. It is called retributive justice. Crime is seen as an act against the State, a law has been broken. The criminal justice system controls the situation. The offender is punished. It is an adversarial relationship. Us against them.

In the Gary Geiger and Wayne Blanchard case, an attempt was made to restore a sense of justice for all involved. This process is called restorative justice. Gary Geiger was allowed to be involved in the dialogue of the mediation. Wayne Blanchard was able to take full responsibility for his actions and be accountable to the victim of his crime. Both could focus on the future.

Although Wayne Blanchard struggles to make it on parole, an incident occurred that points directly to an effort on his behalf to restore justice to his community. Wayne was riding his cousin's bike near the Martin Luther King

Community Center in Albany, New York, when he heard shots ring out. He looked up and saw a car with two passengers shooting at a person walking down the sidewalk. It was a drive by shooting. Wayne recognized the shooter and the wheelman. He had hung out with them in the local park in his youth. What does he do: nothing or notify the police of the perpetrators? What had prompted the drive by shooting was a confrontation a day earlier. Two people were heading towards the same parking place.

One pulled his car into the space before the other. The second man got out of his car and demanded the space. He was greeted by the first man and a gun. The man stated that this was his "mother fucking" parking spot and he fired a round up in the air. The second man agreed that, indeed, this was the man's "mother fucking" parking spot and he carefully got back into his car and drove off; however, he drove over to his uncle's crib and told him that he had been "dissed"(disrespected) by the other party and had been put down in front of a number of people near the youth center. This lack of respect could not be tolerated and the man and his uncle climbed into his car and drove back to the scene. The other party, a known player in the hood, was nowhere to be found.

A day later, the man and his uncle were again cruising around and they spotted the guilty party walking down the street. They drove up to him and the uncle unloaded his gun into "the dissor." Wayne Blanchard saw the whole thing. Before Wayne could make up his mind about what to do about the incident, he was revoked again for not going to his counseling program and testing positive for marijuana. Sitting behind bars he began to think about what he had seen. Was it time for him to begin to restore justice in his community? Interestingly enough, he contacted Gary Geiger and Tom Christian and asked for their advice. Tom Christian had just read the weekly *Sunday Parade Maga-*

zine and the front cover showed Jim Brown, the former football great and now movie actor, dressed in his African garb. The article went on to say that the Black man, in general, had to stand up in his community and be the husband to his wife and the father to his children and begin to turn around his neighborhood and community. Jim Brown had not always been the greatest role model, but this time his words hit home.

Wayne was advised that he had two choices. One was to do nothing because he would be seen as a" snitch." His second option was to come forward and testify against the two perpetrators and be a stand up man in his community. He had heard through the streets that the shooter had shot someone else in the past for similar reasons. This was his chance to help his community get rid of a predator who did not respect life. The police and the district attorney's office were notified that an eyewitness to the drive by shooting was willing to testify. The police were skeptical, and Wayne was asked to write out exactly what he saw and whom he saw do the shooting. Wayne followed through and wrote the detailed letter. It was determined that Wayne was, indeed, at the scene of the shooting. The information he provided was not only accurate but very believable, down to the driver and the shooter. The police, up to that time, had no idea who was responsible for the killing or where to find them. But Wayne knew.

Gary Geiger and Tom Christian sat in the courtroom. On one side was the family and friends of the accused, and on the other side was the family and friends of the victim. Gary and Tom carefully moved to the side of the victim's family. Wayne Blanchard was brought in with leg irons from the correctional facility. He walked down the aisle, hunched over, and swaying back and forth, and took the stand. He knew "Cut" (street name of the shooter) and his nephew, the driver. He calmly told the story, and when the jury heard that Wayne had even smoked "grass" with the accused years before, there was little doubt about his credibility. The defense attorney tried to paint Wayne as just another convict trying to gain his own freedom by his testimony. Wayne said he was not promised an early release from parole. He was doing it to help his community and take a predator off the streets. He had done wrong in the past and it was time to do the right thing. "Cut" was found guilty of second-degree murder and is serving twenty-five to life in the New York State Correctional System. The driver of the car saw the handwriting on the wall and confessed for a lower plea. He knew that Wayne was ready to testify again, this time against him. He wanted no part of a life sentence.

The headlines in the article the next day in the *Albany Times Union* declared, "Felon Seeks Redemption Through Testimony". Wayne Blanchard said in 1981 he had shot a man, and now he felt he could repay society and his community by coming forward and taking a predator off the streets. Wayne Blanchard had experienced restorative justice in the mediation between Gary Geiger and himself and he applied it again during his testimony in the courtroom. The mediation had affected his thinking about crime and victims. Now, he was beginning to apply it to himself. He had a ways to go but he had begun. The family of the victim thanked Wayne and told him how courageous he was to stand up to the pressure to do nothing.

The word spread quickly on the streets. Wayne Blanchard was a "snitch". He had given up a brother to the white establishment. The Black ministers, however, talked to their youth groups and congregations that Sunday and called Wayne Blanchard a real man who was standing up for his community and getting rid of a menace to the Arbor Hill neighborhood. Wayne Blanchard had restored a sense of justice in his own mind and to his community. The positive message was well received by both young and old. Wayne was seen as a role model in a strange kind of way.

Gary Geiger was elated that Wayne Blanchard had not only helped him but was now helping others. Gary began giving talks to local high schools, telling the young people to make good choices in life. He would show the twenty-minute HBO film now called The Gary Geiger Story and discuss his experience with them. He is credited in keeping many young people in school who had contemplated quitting. Many victims' groups and civic groups have asked him to speak to their organizations. Gary Geiger has been responsible for bringing a victim from the Columbine School shooting to Albany to speak to other victims and students. He also brought Tammy Crow, the Olympic athlete, to New York to speak on forgiveness and restorative justice after her serious car accident where two people were killed.

Gary Geiger and Tom Christian have appeared alone and together in schools and community groups and on a number of television and radio shows (for example, Terri Gross's show "Fresh Air" on National Public Radio) speaking about the mediation, crime and restorative justice. Gary Geiger, Wayne Blanchard (out on parole) and Tom Christian have appeared together on the television program, Leeza, and did a presentation together at the Albany Law School. Tom Christian has done training on victim and offender mediation in a number of states and uses the video of the full Gary Geiger and Wayne Blanchard mediation as one of his main training tools.

Gary Geiger located two of the other perpetrators in the 1981 shooting. One was Goldie Jackson whom he met with in another mediation. This mediation took place in New York City at the New York State Court System offices and Tom Christian served again as the mediator. This mediation, with the permission of the parties, was recorded and played on National Public Radio. Gary also met Ramel

A. Eaddy at a boxing match. Ramel was fighting a friend of Gary's, Pat Cavanaugh. After the close fight which Ramel won, Gary talked to Ramel and has since met with him a number of times. Ramel, at the time of this interview, was doing well working for the city of Albany and running his own small business (book store). Gary actually brought Ramel and Wayne Blanchard together to iron out hard feelings between the two because Wayne never resolved the conflict over whether Ramel had given up (testified against) Wayne in the original holdup and trial.

Gary resumed his track career and began to regain his lost speed. He is presently the holder of numerous Masters sprinting records for the Adirondack Region. He has the record for the 55-meter dash, age group 45-49 at the Manley Field House in Syracuse, New York. In 1992, he was the recipient of the Masters Track and Field All American Certificate for 45-49 age group for 100 meters (11.9 seconds). He won the silver second place medal at the 1994 Masters Empire State Games in the 45-49 age group. In 1995 and 1996, he won the 100meter dash at the United States of America Track and Field (USAT&F) meet in the 45-49 age group. In 1996 he also won the 200meter race at the USAT&F Adirondack meet. He was the recipient of All American certificates from 1997-2000 for the 55 through 400 meters. He is ranked first in his age group in the USA for the 55 meters, 2002 indoor season. He is the Gold Medal winner in the 400-meter dash in the 1998 Empire State Senior Games and also the Gold Medal winner in the 100 and 200 meters in the 2000 and 2001 Empire State games. He is the Niagara Association indoor record holder for the 55-meter dash, 50-59 age group (7.0 seconds). In 2003, Gary Geiger was elected to the Capital District Sports Hall of Fame as a senior sprinter. Pat Riley was also inducted into the Hall of Fame as a basketball player and National Basketball Association (NBA) coach. Gary always wanted "to be like Pat" and now they are enshrined together in the same Hall of Fame.

Gary Geiger feels that justice has been restored in his life. His work, his family life, his community involvement, his track achievements, all have given him a sense of peace, accomplishment and satisfaction. He credits it to the mediation that he had with Wayne Blanchard. As a victim, he felt frustrated and angry. Through the restorative experience of being able to talk to Wayne Blanchard, Gary feels renewed. The bullet is still in his body, but it no longer slows him down. In fact, he talks about it in his presentations and he encourages numerous people of all ages to not get mired in self-pity and poor choices. He is an example of a person who not only survived an horrendous experience but one who thrives on the strength he has received from going through this trauma and the mediation, working his way to a positive self-esteem and a healthy outlook on people and life. He has gone from self-pity and post-traumatic stress to an inner strength and a strong desire to help others. For Gary Geiger, justice has truly been restored.

ABOUT THE AUTHOR

THOMAS F. CHRISTIAN retired as the State Director of the Community Dispute Resolution Centers Program for the New York State Unified Court System serving from 1981 through 1996. In 1997, he was presented the Peace Builder Award from the New York State Dispute Resolution Association. Past positions include director of the Alternatives to Incarceration Project for the National Center for State Courts which served twelve southern states, state director of the Minnesota Community Corrections Association, and director of an award winning community-based correctional program. He has worked in correctional institutions and is a former senior probation officer from Hennepin County Court Services in Minneapolis, Minnesota. In 1979, he was voted the Corrections Professional of the Year by the Minnesota Corrections Association.

He has taught at the University of Minnesota and Mankato State University and has lectured at many colleges and universities. He has written extensively in the field of criminal justice. In 1999, he published a book through the American Correctional Association entitled, *Conflict Management and Conflict Resolution in Corrections*.

He has mediated victim and offender cases that have been featured on the CBS Program *48 Hours*, Home Box Office (HBO) and National Public Radio.

He has a master's degree in criminal justice and a doctorate in social science from the School of Criminal Justice at Michigan State University. He is married and has three grown children.

THOMAS F. CHRISTIAN
Mediator, Arbitrator, Trainer
Consultant & Criminal Justice Specialist
35963 Golf Course Drive • Tucson, Arizona 85739-1684
(520) 818-1620 • E-Mail: tanose@aol.com

Printed in the United States
89385LV00002B/37/A